VortexZone

Headphones

ToxicBrain Flask

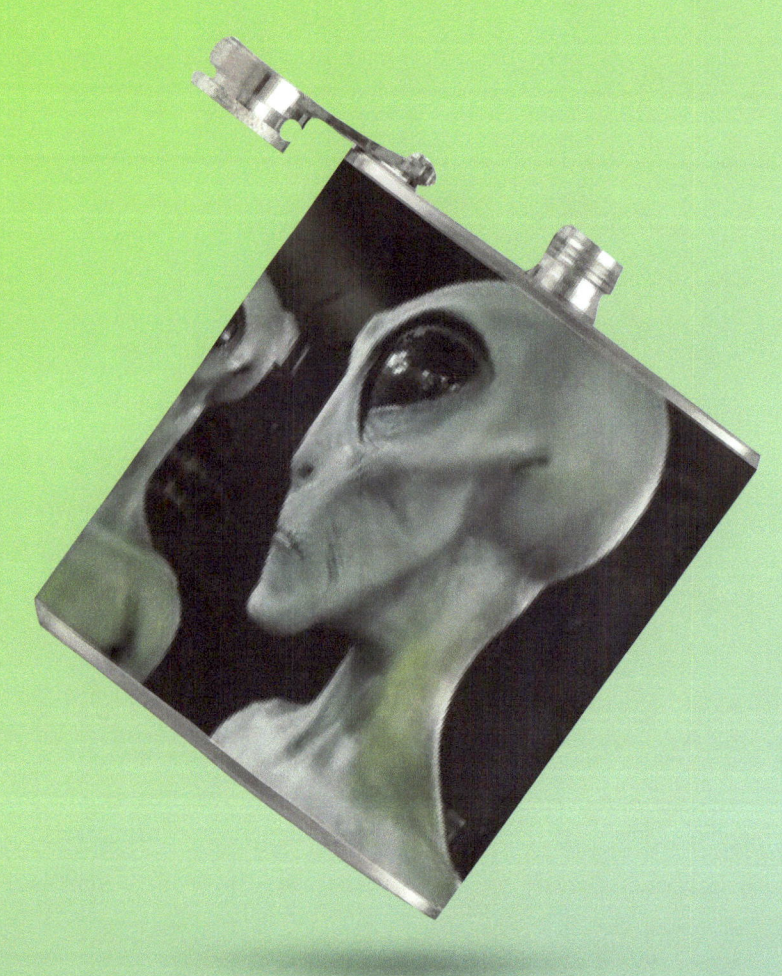

Get Some Alien Brain!
zazzle.com/DistractedMasses

What's Inside:

Feature Article: Teleportation, Time Travel, and the Multiverse

---

The Global Rise of the New Left

Absolutism vs Relativism – Truth in the Making

Poetry, Commentary, Book Reviews, Cool Merchandise, and Much More!

Just Chillin' Aviator Shades

Got dem' irie eyes!

Early 2016

Vol. 1 Issue #4

DISTRACTED MASSES

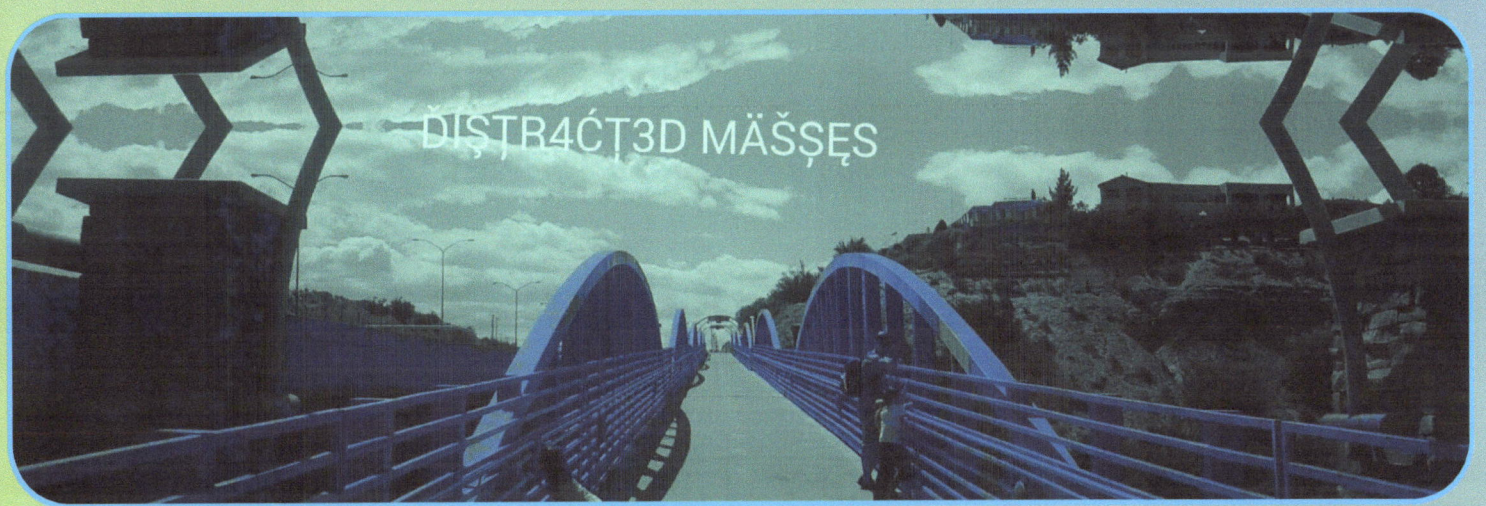

DIŞTR4ĆŢ3D MÄŞŞĘS

Bridge to the Future

How do you manifest your own destiny? Is it giving ourselves to God and saying our leaders are bestowed by God to decide our destiny for us? Or is that just giving in to pre-determinism? I'm a believer in free will and think each human being has the ability to decide the personal events that unfold in life before them for themselves. Yes, external forces will knock people off track and influence the events every individual bears witness to, but that doesn't mean we don't all carry an extremely powerful internal force within our minds and bodies which can also influence the events around us. I doubt humans would've built flying machines if that wasn't true.

The question becomes then, how do we use this force to create the future we desire? How do we combine our own personal desires with those of others to collectively build our universe the way we all want it to be built? Well, all we have to do is look at the Hawaiian third Huna principle of life, *makia,* and that is, "energy goes where energy flows."

So for this issue *Distracted Masses* is embarking on a new journey of discovery to learn exactly how this works. Through this publication the writers will try to figure out where the energy is going by studying the conversations and articles in social and mass media. We will try and learn what people are paying attention to, what people are thinking about

collectively, and how they are reacting to their thoughts. The idea is that the information we consume effects our thoughts, which in turn effects our behaviors. This is where *Distracted Masses* moves beyond media analysis and the discernment of mis- and disinformation. This is where we begin to create our own personal future, and perhaps that of others as well, by creating new information for mass consumption in order to redirect the dialogue onto new probability paths.

We will create poetry, fiction, commentary, and other writing & artwork to help open up new probability paths for ourselves and our readers, with the intent of bringing about new types of change through collective input and mass consciousness. We are believers in multidimensionality: the world is not just black and white. There is no up or down, yes or no final decision. All probability paths remain open for discovery no matter what the present state may seem to restrict us to, no matter how we collapse our wave function.

So join us on this new journey and help dispel the myths of disinfo by manifesting your own new reality! Together we can build a bridge to the future which unites those on similar probability paths, seeking similar goals. Like the root systems of trees we shall branch out widely, but will always stay firm in our quest for new adventure, life, and nourishment. So join us now, and learn what the future beholds . . .

TELEPORTATION, TIME TRAVEL, AND THE MULTIVERSE

By Scott Albright

Theoretical physicist Michio Kaku tells us in his book *Hyperspace* that the 10 dimensional superstring theory may be the key to finding the Theory of Everything. As exciting as this may be, there still seems to be many different interpretations of what each of these dimensions looks like. We're told that moving from the fourth dimension of spacetime up to the fifth would be similar to a 2D flatlander trying to understand the third dimension. Our brains just can't comprehend it because we aren't able to experience it.

We're told that ripples in the fifth dimension could explain how light is created, and yet it could also be another dimension of spacetime that is orthogonal, or at right angles, to the dimension before it. Because spacetime is space and time put together we can understand how the spatial aspect to the fourth dimension can be measured. The fourth dimension is not just a temporal representation of the past, present, and future, but also all those places in which the past, present, and future have existed or will exist in the future, meaning these places are in a real and precise physically existent temporal and spatial location. They don't just exist in the present, but they are a physical reality of the present, past, and future.

This makes sense if you think of human beings as a frequency or embodiment of energy vibrating at different wavelengths and energy levels. These vibrations effect our perception of time - how fast or slow it appears to be moving relative to others - and in turn, effects the reality of our spacetime experience. For example, the rate at which time seems to pass for someone in prison is going to be very different for someone living life freely about on the outside.

Our vibrational energy allows us to move through time at different speeds and allows us to connect with other creatures and objects who are also moving at different speeds and times. Our connection to each other allows us to interact along different parts of the spacetime continuum which spans across the past, present, and future. Our own bodies and minds also spans across the continuum of past, present, and future. However, our biological core, or our solid state of being, seems to only exist in the same present state as all the rest of the solid objects in the universe. They are within the same frequency and in synchronicity, or alignment, with the other energies in the universe in one single present state. But our minds don't move as fast as this frequency.

Our minds have to process all the information on this frequency level before we can make sense of it. In other words, our present state of conscious being is in a past state relative to the rest of our body, or biological core. Our bodies absorb the vast amounts of information pulsating on the present state of physicality through our different senses and filter out everything we don't need. Billions of bits of information are discarded, with humans only taking in that which can help us make our next conscious decision in life. But we make this decision in the past relative to when the information we processed was first sensed or absorbed, sometimes waiting days, weeks, or even years before making a final choice based on the information we've received. But there is still a connection between the information from the present and the information in one's past state. And here we get turned around, for what is really the past state if you are in the future from when you last received the information you make a decision on? Just because our conscious state is in the past relative to our biological core doesn't mean it can't make a decision at a later time in the future. This connection bet-

Alien Mantis Shirt - $27.40

-ween our past, present, and future allows us to live in a four dimensional world, but still our biological core seems to be locked in a present state, no matter how far our mental state is in the past or future from it. Now there are anti-aging drugs which can take our biological core back to a past state as well, so there is a spatial and temporal measuring stick we can use to find exactly where we are in the universe, but still nobody is taking their bodies back to 1987, as far as I know, so this measuring stick is limited in its usefulness.

Observation is key though. How do we "collapse the wave function", so to speak, in order to "see" a present state in which the future and past states are more than just imaginary places? Well, we have to visualize the right angles to our third dimensional space, but those right angles are impossible to comprehend because we can't see them. They are outside our purview. We are just flatlanders unable to experience this other dimension in spacetime. And this is just the fourth dimension! Really existing in the fourth dimension requires us to be able to not just travel between fractions of seconds of past, present, and future states mentally and physically, but it would mean we should be able to also physically take our bodies back as far as Medieval times or the time of the dinosaurs and view and experience these places in space and time from a conscious present state. It would mean that there exists right now an Earth that has not yet orbited the sun the same number of times as the Earth I am sitting on here. It means that other place in the Earth's timeline or probability path is at some right angle to the third dimensional space around me at the moment I am writing this. This is truly hard to believe, and until I can access these places and live there myself I won't

believe it to be true, but that doesn't mean we shouldn't stop exploring these areas further.

Truly existing in the fourth dimension would mean we should be able to teleport ourselves and other objects. We know that an object we want to send is going to get to the place we send it to, but using our current technology we're not always sure how long it will take to get there. Theoretically, to get the object there faster all we would have to do is move it at specific right angles from its current position in spacetime and it should be able to arrive at its destination instantaneously, as we know that a straight path to it is not always the fastest route, so a quicker path must exist, which is through the fourth dimension. In essence, the object moves to a future state that already exists within our present state and gets there by moving through the fastest route in the fourth dimension. The object would exist in two places at the same time for a fraction of a second, connecting space and time in ways which make both teleportation and time travel possible. Basically, the object moves to a place in space that is in a future time relative to the senders but in a present state relative to those observing the object when it arrives at its final destination. In many ways this is similar to how we observe our own biological core, which is in a future state relative to our mental conscious present.

But beyond the connection between our conscious and biological core states, how does the past, present, and future exist all at the same time? Well, anti-time. Time doesn't just move forward. It moves backwards too, it's just that we have a hard time perceiving the existence of this backward moving time because of our position relative to it. Our view of it restricts us to a certain perspective which makes us believe we are only in one state, the present, which means we can only be in one place, or wherever we are in the present, which is seemingly always moving toward the future, or in a continuous forward-like one-directional motion. To have a wider view we need to scale our perspective up so as to get a better understanding of how things look from an outside observer, and to see the reality of the motion of objects, mass, and energy around us. What I do is imagine the planet spinning around in one direction as it falls toward the sun, realizing the sun's two hemispheres spin in opposite directions as it also falls toward the center of the Milky Way. I picture the Earth's own electromagnetic field, thinking of it as a rotating toroidal sphere of liquid metal emanating energy lines out from and back into it's central core. I think of how the Earth tilts back and forth as it spins and orbits around the sun, causing our own hemispheres to have different seasons at the same time. I imagine the energies from the sun, the earth, and our own biological cores as torus fields, swirling in all directions of infinity in perfect harmony and balance. I imagine the Earth connected to the sun's energy through the light of day, and the sun and Earth's connection to a massively dense rotating toroidal black hole at the center of our galaxy through the darkness of night. These connections are the ripples from the fifth and higher dimensions which allow us to exist in the reality we do relative to one another. They give us meaning and solidify our own place in the universe. But, they are still just relative connections.

The stars we see from Earth are millions of light years away. The light hitting our eyes from those stars was produced before our own existence, allowing us to see the universe in it's past state. We live in the past when we observe that light, and we are in the future relative to that light's original state, yet still only in the present. We become connected between past, present, and future on a universal scale, but yet that doesn't seem to change the fact that our biological core is still only in the present. You still age one year at the same speed I age one year, at least in my own head

anyway, so how can these past and future states really exist? Why can't I just see these past and future states as solid forms and go and live there physically and mentally in my own conscious present state?

What we're told is that perhaps we already do, but we just don't recognize it. What we're told is we need to access the fifth dimension and fold our four dimensional spacetime up in it in order to teleport or time travel to these other existences in spacetime. And this fifth dimension is just at right angles to the fourth, so it shouldn't be too hard to do. Visually, what we see is an arrow of spacetime, all your physical existences in the past, present, and future, until you die, all as one place in space, all existing simultaneously and connected physically. This is what the fourth dimension looks like. This is your probability path of life. Looking back you see the most probable path you took to get where you are now, and up front you see multiple paths of where you are most probabilistically going to go in the future, with all future paths ending at your death (perhaps one loops around back to your birth?). From your present perspective you can consciously only be on one path at a time, so you have to make decisions based on the information you process from the past in order to move forward through that time (and space). Every time you collapse the wave function you are in essence making a decision. You are deciding what you are going to observe now and next, as well as what you have already observed, for what you observe now may connect your future probability paths with probability paths from the past which weren't connected to your original path, in essence changing history as you know it. What you observe now also decides where you will be next along your probability path. At each point along these paths there are multiple, perhaps infinite, amounts of observations you can make, providing further branches along your probability paths of where you may consciously and physically exist sometime in the future. All of these branches and all of these options existing all at once in one chunk of spacetime is the fifth dimension, so we're told. This is the many worlds interpretation.

The many worlds interpretation tells us there

are infinite amounts of you existing in infinite parts of the universe all at the same time(s), and all connected in some way or another which should provide us access to those places. This is also the basis of the holographic principle, which states all the information we observe in the universe exists within every single bit of the rest of the information around us. So the tiniest subatomic particle contains all of the information of the universe within it, like there is some type of universal DNA or code that exists within everything which can tell us about everything else in the universe. The whole universe is just a piece of information smeared across itself, and we too are smeared across this holographic universe, or multiverse, in space and time, but conscious and able to observe our own existence in the present state of the third and fourth dimensions. Somewhere, someplace out there, there may be an infinite amount of us smeared across the different dimensions as conscious informational beings unaware of the rest of our own existences. Unfortunately, our consciousness and biological core restricts us to being in just one place at a time, so even if we do travel to a another place in the multiverse where we exist in the past or future, or some other strange version of the present, we wouldn't recognize that we'd traveled there. The chances are we'd only take the most probable path to get there, which would mean the place we go to would look exactly like the last place we left, and even if it looked completely different, there's a chance we wouldn't remember the last place we were because there would be no history of ever existing in the new place in the multiverse, so your consciousness would have to rely on the history of the other you which already existed in that part of the universe prior to you arriving there. That history would be the memory you most probabilistically would think of as your own. In turn, that would be your new reality, which would cause you to think you had always existed in that part of the multiverse, unless your were some way able to combine the two memories of the two conscious yous as they simultaneously existed in one body. But how would that be possible, and what type of technology would be needed to help you get there? Well, let's figure that out.

If another you consciously exists in another part of the universe, say ten years from now, and you somehow are able to consciously move from your present state to that future you instantaneously, where does the other conscious you from that part of the multiverse go? Is consciousness just energy that transfers to different parts of your probability path, moving the consciousness that existed there prior to you arriving to another branch along that path? Does each collapse of the wave function bump another physical and conscious existence of you further along a different part or branch of the probability path? Is it possible for you to meet the other you, or do the laws of physics prohibit these two conscious energy states from existing on the same part of the same probability path? Well I guess it depends on how probable you think it is and if you can move along a path, or make observations, which make that conclusion even more probable or likely to occur than before.

Some say meditation, hallucinogenic drugs, extreme physical exercise, or some form of mental illness might allow us to access these parts of the universe, where another you exists, where a dreamlike lucid world is not just fantasy, but real. It is very probable you will experience a different reality using these different methods to consciously observe the world around you, and there is also a probable outcome which says one of the methods of observation may lead the observer to believe the observation is real, or is indeed the reality they exist in. On LSD someone might turn their hallucination into a reality, physically sensing the illusory world, smelling, touching, and tasting it. A yogi may visualize they're younger selves also meditating before them, or maybe they're capable of bringing on an out of body experience where they travel to different parts of the multiverse, making it feel as though it were a real and physical experience. Maybe a schizophrenic has visions of living in a reality no one else can see. For these people it is real, even if only momentarily, but

these other realities are not the standard.

These methods are too personalized, only relative to the individual, imprecise, and lacking organization or standard logic for others to understand as meaningful ways to experience the rest of reality. It is too chaotic for us to adopt as a way for building future transport systems, and too surreal or non-physical for it to work in a way which can meet all of our basic human needs.

But what if there was another way to prove these other realities do in fact exist? What if we could map out all the probability paths of our past and future selves based on all the information we had available to us in the present? What if we could measure the right angles of the higher dimensions and see that each collapse of the wave function is not just one conscious existence, but a multitude of infinite existences that don't just live as possibilities, but as probabilities? What if we learned how to manipulate the probabilities of wave function collapse so that we could change the way we observe our own present state? What if there was a technology out there that allowed us to enfold our four dimensional world into the fifth dimension, allowing us to teleport or time travel across the universe, or multiverse? What would that technology look like and how would it work?

This is where the aliens come in. If extraterrestrials are advanced enough to visit Earth, as many claim has occurred, than they would've had to create a transport system that moves the occupants extremely fast. It means they would have to have a technology which allows them to teleport across star systems, and of course if they can teleport they can time travel, because they are moving from a past state to a future state instantaneously, allowing them to traverse millions of light years worth of spacetime to get to wherever or whenever they'd like to go. So how would they do this? By accessing and learning to manipulate fourth, fifth, and possibly higher dimensions, of course. They would have to create a machine that can bend the four dimensional space time around them at precise right angles to their present physical and temporal locations which allow them to transport themselves to another place in the multiverse - a place they had mapped out beforehand and programmed into their machine. This machine would have to be able to withstand impacts with other solid objects and would have to be able to carry what or whoever it was transporting inside. It would have to create a bubble effect around the occupants in which their conscious observation of spacetime was not effected by the frequencies of external forces outside the machine. It would have to produce

an energy that could warp those frequencies so that the occupants inside were able to change what they observed on the outside depending on how they warped those frequencies using the energy from their machine.

A YouTube video uploaded by videofan88 explains that UFOs may be able to do this by using a technology to warp those frequencies, or the spacetime around them, using something called a Rodin coil. The coil produces an electromagnetic energy that works similar to the toroidal forces we see produced in the planets, stars, and black holes across the universe. This coil, videofan88 tells us, powers the donut shaped UFOs by creating its own hyperspace. Some form of mercury or exotic metal spins around inside the donut shaped craft, moving by the forces of the

the Rodin coil, helping to somehow accelerate the creation of this hyperspace. Spacetime inside this craft would be the present state for the occupants, while on the outside it would be whatever they wanted it to be. They would be creating an energy that moved in such a way and at a such a level that it would warp the spacetime outside the craft, and depending on how they programmed the craft, they could determine where and when in spacetime they wanted the craft to go.

With such a craft time travel and teleportation could be standardized. We could transport ourselves to wherever we wanted to go without there being any dispute as to wether or not we actually went to where we said we did. Everyone could experience it for themselves in the same standard way and there would be no confusion as to who's experience was relative to what. Such a machine would provide organization, preciseness, accuracy, and standardization for future transport systems. Integrated programming would allow these crafts to transport living things and objects to anywhere in the multiverse without interfering with someone else's travels. All probability paths would be mapped and all craft preprogrammed to avoid impacting other craft or objects along the probability paths they chose to travel along, a sort of futuristic air traffic control system. The concept might be difficult to comprehend, and if made available would probably be kept secret by the military for as long as possible, but it does not mean it won't or can't exist, and perhaps it already does.

Thousands of strange spherical orbs, discs, donut, and cigar shaped craft have been observed across the globe in which witnesses say they move from one point in the sky to the next without traversing the space in between. They claim these craft move at extraordinary speeds and military pilots have even chased them, only for the strange craft to evade their pursuit. I have even spotted strange lights in the sky myself and have talked to many people who have also seen flying discs or glowing orbs, or who knows someone who has. Of course these sighting are not

enough to be proof, but there are so many from enough credible witnesses that we can't say it isn't a reality for these witness at least, and possibly, or probabilistically, for the rest of the population as well.

Of course we need more than just sightings to say we have the proof though. We need the occupants or operators of these crafts to communicate with us in the public sphere. We need more than just disclosure, we need the proof in the pudding, and if the proof won't be brought to us from elsewhere in the universe, we'll have to go and find it ourselves. We'll have to build the machine that allows us to access and manipulate these other dimensions. We'll have to keep making the decisions along our probability paths which make the creation of such a machine more probable. We'll have to consciously go where no one else has dared to go, and we'll have to go there together. For as long as such manipulation of the other dimensions remains but a military secret or a personal journey of a lone scientist, it will never be the underlying reality of the masses. We will never know what is beyond the existence of our third and limited fourth dimensional purviews of the universe around us if we don't all embark on the adventure together. So we can wait for the next orb to come down to Earth and show us how to do it, or we can start building our own machine now. Which probability path do you think we should take? Should we wait for the aliens to come to us, or should we become the aliens ourselves?

References/Further Reading

1. Kaku, Michio. *Hyperspace: A Scientific Odyssey Through Parallel Universes, Time Warps, and the 10th Dimension,* Anchor, 1995. http://amzn.to/1LbcBea.
2. 10thdim. "Imagining the Fifth Dimension," YouTube. Uploaded Nov. 17, 2011. https://youtu.be/eN24Sv0qS1w.
3. Spirit Science 21. "Toroidal Flow," YouTube. Uploaded Nov. 6, 2012. https://youtu.be/1-4zdmd0TNU.
4. videofan88. "UFO-Flying Saucer Engine-how it works, YouTube. Uploaded Dec. 14, 2008. https://youtu.be/EeX1v6IZC5g.
5. 3dload. "Helmholtz Torus UFO Technology Ferrofluid Rotor," YouTube. Uploaded Feb. 15, 2010. https://youtu.be/1-tHRDkfWdE.
6. Time Travel. http://time-travelers.org/.
7. Anderson Institute. "Time Travel." http://www.andersoninstitute.com/time-travel.htm.

DIAMOND LOTUS

SHOWER CURTAIN

ZAZZLE.COM/DISTRACCTEDMASSES

ZAZZLE.COM/DISTRACCTEDMASSES

[ColorBoard Bandanna](#) – **$16.85**

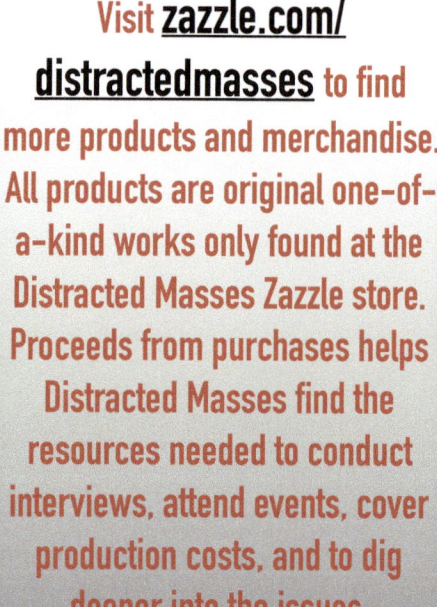

[Metallic Horn Poster](#) – **$7.36**

[Time Swirl Wristwatch](#) – **$48.50**

CHAOS

Where did the canvas go?
I can't see!
Dreaming of infinity. . . .
Deliver me.
Into another reality.

Into the daze.
Slice, faze.
Me again.
Dripping in the sun.

Badlands

Bad sand.
Afghan.
Blast them.
Into never nowhere.
Again.
Friend.

Or brother.
Sister.
Other culture.
Dimension.
Animal.
Beast.

I am,
One.
From,
Planet Earth.

Hatred.
Love.
Drums.
Into the night.
They fight.
For power.

Both win.
In the end.
Sick.
Enough.
To make sick souls,
Vomit & piss Jesus.

And fret forever.
Anxiously.

Run for cover.
In bomb shelter.
Swimming.
In trailer trash.

Redneck.
Republican.
Trumpian.
Thumpin'
In Alabama.
Deep south.
Ignorant,
Stuff out of their mouth.

Untouchable Collaboration

By the blah blah.
For the blah blah blah.
Into blah la.
Land.

And.
Every other inter-dimension.
And place.
Time,
Fold.
Into the mind.

Neuropathways.
We climb.
Into the skies.
Drive.
People off the edge.

Of deceit.
They creep.
The mayor.
The governor.
Her people.
Cronyism.
Sheeple.
Off the cliff .

We go.
All of us.
Even the intelligent.
Insolent.
Belligerent.
Dissident.

They hate us all.
Death.
To our kind.
And rise again.
My friend.
My brother.

We live in wonder.
Mass hallucination.
Hypnotic.
Media.
Create apathy.
For the peasantry.

UpsideDownsized

Marginalized,
Downsized,
Small fries,
See large lies.

Pushed aside,

No voice,
No choice.

But can't be a prisoner for life.
Rise!
Death isn't an option.
See through the lies!
No matter how noxious.
Hear the battle cries!

Make your choice,
Raise your voice!

Stand astride.

Truth to counter lies.
Make them fry.
And never be outsized.
Or marginalized.

Short
How many,
Versions do we get?
Is this it?
Is there no other path?
Probabilistically there's more,
Just dot the math.

The Global Rise of the New Left

The fear of socialism among America's right wing conservatives is almost as great as the fear of the the far right among America's liberals, but no matter who is to be most feared, it's clear there is something big happening on the left that can't be ignored. On the global front there is a continuous anti-austerity pro-worker movement that is still struggling in an uphill battle against the conservative pro-austerity powerbrokers embedded in the various financial institutions and political agencies which give them the ability to crush the hopes and aspirations of the poor and middle class. The opposition is varied in its approach to the challenges they face, but the picture is clear enough to see there is a new left willing to take on the challenges before them, and they aren't scared anymore.

In Greece we see the rise of the leftist Syriza party and it's willingness to challenge the pro-austerity measures presented to Greece's government by the European Troika. Even though the party will inevitably be forced to eat whatever measures the banks inflict upon them, there will still be a continued push by Syriza to work with political partners throughout Europe to pressure the banks to improve financial and economic conditions for their countries. From the rise of Podemos in Spain to the

Corbynmania of the UK, and the Blockupy movement throughout Europe, all the way across the Atlantic where the right wing is beginning to #FeelTheBern, it's not

Katja Kippling, Alex Tsipiras, Bernie Sanders, Jeremy Corbyn, Iglesias. Image source: Wikimedia Commons & Wikipedia.

hard to tell there is a global movement that is far different from any we've seen before. This is not a Russian or Chinese-backed pro-communist global revolutionary movement. This is not a peasant or worker uprising. This is a movement directly caused by the failed policies of the pro-austerity powerbrokers who have continued to make the rich and powerful even more rich and powerful while trampling on the rights and lives of millions of hard working middle class and poor citizens of the world. This a movement, a global movement, brought to you by the people who've decided they've had enough. Not just the poor, uneducated, and working class, but also the intellectuals, the white collar workers, the educated, and the young and old alike. It is a movement of the 99%. A 99% who

are sick and tired of being forced to work impossible hours for minimal pay in order to qualify for more debt that they have to have just to get by. Just to pay for school. Just to have a roof over their heads. Just to have food in their bellies. They are tired of being debt slaves, imprisoned by their financial masters. And they are starting to rise up.

The media and right wing conservative pundits are already baking up batches of paranoid political pie for the masses in order to scare their audiences away from the movement, but so far that hasn't seemed to work. The anti-austerity rallies in England may not draw as large of audiences as the Bernie Sanders' rallies in the U.S., but that doesn't mean they aren't big. And combined, Blockupy, Podemos, and Syriza will certainly keep Merkel and her ECB counterparts on their toes. It's the real deal, and if you aren't paying attention, maybe you should.

In the U.K. Jeremy Corbyn, an anti-war, anti-austerity leftist, took over the Labour Party's leadership positions in a landslide election where he won almost 60% of the vote. In Greece, Tsipiras' Syriza Party has risen to power on a similar platform, and in Spain Podemos' Iglesias has done the same thing, while in Germany Katja Kippling's Left Party is on the rise despite being under surveillance by the Bundesamt fur Verfassungsschutz (domestic intelligence) for their "extremist" socialist democratic ideals. The Left (Die Linke) is the third largest parliamentary group among the four groups in the German Bundestag, having held 64 of the 630 seats after the 2013 federal elections. Although political analysts point out that the rise in popularity of the xenophobic anti-immigration party Alternative for Germany (AfD) will pose challenges for Die Linke in it's ability to build winning coalitions in some parts of the country, it probably will have little effect on its ability to join up with and reinvigorate the Social Democratic Party of Germany (SPD) in a three-party coalition with the Greens. Judith Meyer writes in her "German Parties' Outlook 2016" article that, "For SPD, it would be good to at least have the possibility of threatening this kind of coalition, in order not to lose influence within the Grand Coalition until 2017. This may mean replacing the current SPD-CDU coalition in Berlin state with an SPD-Linke one later this year."

When it comes to building global coalitions among the left there are many common characteristics between the different political parties, not just in Europe and North America, but all across South and Central America and many other parts of the world as well. Of course parties shift in ideologies - left eventually becomes right, and right becomes left - but at the moment there is a common leftist platform of anti-austerity/debt reduction, pro-spending on social programs, a focus on improving the financial well being of the poor and middle class, as well as a pro-environment/anti-war focus. Germany's Die Linke may be more extreme in it's use of language regarding its anti-war policies than Sanders, or other leading leftist politicians, ever will be, but the sentiment is similar throughout. Die Linke's leader in the Bundestag, Sahra Wagenknecht, is quoted as saying, "Of course, it is no lesser crime to murder civilians in Syria with bombs than to open fire at random in restaurants and concert halls in Paris." The more centrist Corbyn is a little less dramatic in his anti-war approach, but he still says things like "I was appalled that MPs should clap, shout and cheer when we were deciding to go and bomb somewhere," while in Canada newly elected leftist Prime Minister Justin Trudeau has called for an end to Canada's role in carrying out airstrikes in Syria. Sanders, on the other hand, supports airstrikes against ISIS, despite being outspoken about previous administrations' "failed" war policies in the Middle East. But for Sanders, moving any further to the left on issues of war and finance could be disastrous for his campaign, no matter which coalition partners he may lose.

U.S. foreign policy has typically been pro-right/anti-leftist, partially due to old Cold War military policies, but mostly due to the greed of bankers and financial elitists who prosper from right-wing free trade policies, conservative western-style international banking systems, and the propping up of (rightist) foreign governments that are open to total privatization of their country's resources. Those who have worked against the right-wing policies of the international banksters have been assassinated, lost their jobs, or have just disappeared. What the new left represents is a direct threat to these banksters, who we can expect to react the same way they always have - violently. Syriza, Blockupy, Podemos, Corbyn, and Sanders will all be shunned by the mainstream media, which are owned by these international banksters, and will have to fight hard to get into the minds of the people. Sanders is already saying that Wall Street is not going to like him, and anyone who's followed U.S. politics knows that that is a sure way to not get elected - being opposed to corrupted money - but that's the platform he's running on and people love it. Not the rich and super rich, but normal everyday people who have suffered time and again from the failed economic policies of these international banksters. So Sanders does still have a chance, but even if he is elected I don't know how much he'll be allowed to get away with. Even his idea of postal banking might be too much for the banksters to handle. Any president who attempts to give government back the job of issuing it's own currency or putting any type of banking operation under the guise of government will likely be blocked at every turn, although eventually all governments will end up owing so much debt to these banksters there will be no way to pay it all off other than by printing their own money, however that is still a ways off. In the meantime, we can expect Venezuela's Central Bank to be taken out of public control and given over to the bankers, after economic collapse, social disruptions, and most likely much violence, that is. We also can expect Islamic banking, which outlaws usury, to be wiped out completely, with Iran at the center of the banksters target, as it is too much to allow Iran to control their own money. And there is precedent for this, such as when Iran's democratically elected president Mohammed Mossadegh was overthrown with the help of British and U.S. intelligence operatives, simply because he nationalized the country's oil after being elected (BP and their financial backers didn't like this). If there is a state owned banking system, the international banksters will try and seize it. They need to control all aspects of the market, particularly a nation's currency.

Giving government, and the people it represents, that much control over their own money or resources (oil, gold, uranium, etc.) would be too much for the banksters. Sanders is lucky he hasn't been seriously threatened by them already, but if he's smart he can manage the threats, which are bound to come full throttle if he continues to try and take on Wall Street. Some journalists and commentators have already speculated that a bullet hole found in the window of a Sanders' campaign headquarters in Las Vegas, Nevada was evidence of an assassination attempt. PollyReed, an online commentator discussing the bullet hole, writes that Sanders "has to request SS [Secret Service] protection which he hasn't done though he meets all the requirements to have it. It cost the taxpayer $48,000/day for that and that might be why he hasn't asked." And then, almost as a second thought, the commentator writes, "Given the history of the SS, I think he is better off without it, seriously." From the research I've done so far, I might just have to agree.

One of the first things Sander's will have to do is revamp the Secret Service so it actually serves his own safety interests (just renaming it might help, as the abbreviation SS is associated with the Nazi Schutzstaffel, or the Protection Squadron. Some U.S. Marines also brand SS into their arms, standing for Scout Sniper). At least one former Secret Service member has already publicly denounced Sanders, essentially calling his Democratic Socialist ideas a threat to the (free-market) economy. Clearly these are not the people Sanders should use for personal protection, especially when some are publicly already in favor of protecting the private war banksters ideologies than an actual human being who seeks to take some of that abusively violent power away from them. No, the Secret Service was not set up to protect people like Sanders.

The original mission of the Secret Service was to combat counterfeiting, starting in 1865, and later took on the role of presidential protection, but not before the Federal Reserve took over the job of printing out and lending bank notes to the U.S. government. The Secret Service was later transferred from the Department of Treasury to the Department of Homeland Security, but the mission has remained the same - protecting the president and investigating financial crimes - crimes the banks have continued to get away with despite all the evidence against them. In reality, the Secret Service is designed more to protect the banks than it is the president, and if Sanders were president he would need protection against the banks, something the Secret Service is unable to do given the length of time at which the bankers have had to infiltrate and rig the Fed, the Department of Treasury, Homeland Security, and the Secret Service all in their favor. So just staying alive and out of the scope of the economic hitmen and banksters will be a big job in itself for Sanders, but that would just be the beginning. Revamping the Secret Service, appointing board members to the Fed that are in alignment with Sanders' economic policies, re-enacting Glass-Steagall, breaking up the monopoly big banks have on the financial sector, and reining in Wall Street may not be something that can be done in four years. The financial elite have embedded themselves into every party of Washington politics - they influence economic policy, military policy, and social policies through their agents, lobbyists, and provocateurs who take advantage of the D.C. - Wall Street revolving door our politicians have left wide open for the sake of the rich and super rich. Yes indeed, Sanders will not have any easy ride if he is elected.

But he should be elected, as should all of the other leftists running on the anti-austerity platform we see around the world today. The banksters have truly taken advantage of the everyday people, from those in the slums of India to the factories of China, and even in the so-called industrialized western countries of Europe and North America. They have a stranglehold on the entire economy and if nobody is willing to do anything they will only tighten their death grip. Sure, there is the possibility of them trying to kill our future president or starting a huge war to finance more debt schemes to keep them in power and their companies more profitable, but either way it's a lose-lose situation. Doing nothing is a sure pathway to more mediocrity, poverty, and almost-but-not-quite type of lifestyles. People need financial security, economic surety, and a system that can make it all more possible. What we have now isn't working, and it's sure to get worse if we let it, so I'm all on board for making sure we don't just get walked on some more. And by the look of the polls I've seen, it seems like a lot of other people are on board too.

The official polls show that Sanders is very popular and only a few points behind Hillary Clinton in the Iowa presidential caucus, but most of the official polls rarely have sample sizes over 1,500. To get a better understanding of how popular he really is, we turn to a Twitter poll by Black Lives Matter activist

Derry Mckesson. In a Nov. 14, 2015 poll Mckesson asked his followers, "If you voted tomorrow, who would vote for to be the next President of the United States?" Out of the two candidates listed, 83 percent of the 42,575 voters preferred Sanders. I believe Mckesson's sample size is not only much larger than most of the official polls, but also more indicative of the national sentiment (but perhaps not of actual future results). But as we all know from past rigging of the U.S. election system, polls, and even votes, aren't always a good representation of reality. I have yet to see a pro-Trump, pro-Bush, or pro-Clinton sign or bumper sticker anywhere around where I live, yet I've seen tons of pro-Sanders signs and bumper stickers, so from my perspective the reality is that Sanders is much more popular than the mainstream media will ever let on.

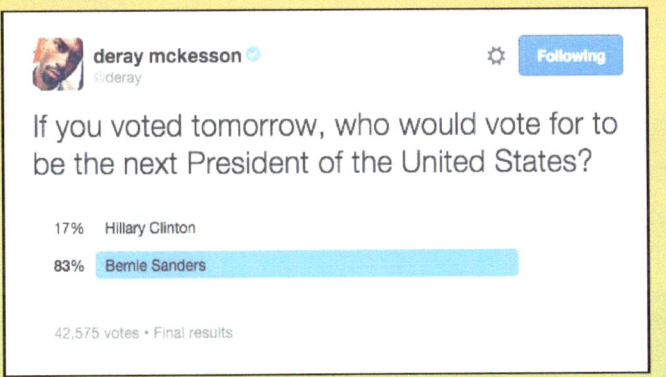

Despite the popularity of Sanders and the new left, there are some slippery slopes ahead. The more traction the leftists build, the easier those slopes will be to climb out of. And now is the time to gain more traction. There are seats to be won worldwide, coalitions to be built, and generations to be won over. Party politics is what we have, and it's how we operate today, so there is no shame in saying #UniteBlue even if you are scared of socialism. Plenty of countries have democratic socialist systems and the people living there are prosperous, well educated, peaceful, clean, modernized, happy, and socially satisfied. No one's saying we should bring the banks to their knees and make them scream mercy. What the leftists are saying is that there are alternative ways to the type of economic system we now have, which only gives those who can operate at an economy of scale any chance of competing in the real life games of Risk and Monopoly these banksters are playing.

What the left is saying is that we should even the playing field so that everyone can all be better off, economically and socially. There is security in this for all, and I don't understand why anyone would be against making the world safer and more economically sound. Sure, people profit from disasters & conflicts, and paranoid politics has become the norm, but even the banksters know you can only push the limit so far before things get out of control. The social disruptions caused by the failed economic policies of trickle down economics and profit before people has devastated entire countries. As the technologies we use become more deadly and the populations larger, it will become inevitable that the scale of destruction will grow as we continue to drive on the same paths we've been down before. I even understand why the rich and super rich would want to exploit workers and force feed the masses disinformative propaganda to build brand loyalty and so forth, but it's beginning to wear on the people. Anyone who's travelled overseas will notice the same nationalistic propaganda sold at the stores. They're practically all owned by the same companies and they're all out there pushing ethnocentric, divisive thought control toys and goods for our consumption. This is done on purpose, but the people are beginning to see through it.

What's strange though is how similar the right and left actually are when it comes to economic policy. Tea Party libertarians want to balance the budget, audit the Fed, and empower entrepreneurs and small business owners. From all indicators, it appears the left wants the same thing. So even in a two party system like that in the U.S., there are factions within the parties, and new coalitions to be built. Yes, there are still huge differences among those factions, and yes, paranoid politics will have everyone flipping sides periodically, but in the end there are common goals and objectives all parties can agree on and which *must* be accomplished. However, in the global political landscape it appears as though the left is the only faction pushing for a common goal, at least for the poor, middle class, oppressed, and disenfranchised, otherwise known as the majority of the people. This is why I believe the global rise of the new left is not only necessary, but also an act of public service that will benefit the most amount of people in the most amount of places at one time.

www.distractedmasses.weebly.com

References

1. Dathan, Matt and Jon Stone. "The 9 charts that show the policies of Jeremy Corbyn the public actually agrees with," *Independent,* July 23, 2015. http://www.independent.co.uk/news-14-5/the-jeremy-corbyn-policies-that-most-people-actually-agree-with-10407148.html.
2. http://www.bbc.com/news/uk-politics-34221155
3. Stratford Global Intelligence. German Political Parties Plan for the Future, Nov. 10, 2015. https://www.stratfor.com/image/german-political-parties-plan-future.
4. Project Gutenberg Self-Publishing Press. "The Left (Germany)", sourced from World Heritage Encyclopedia, accessed Dec. 25, 2015. http://self.gutenberg.org/articles/the_left_(germany)#cite_note-Netzeitung-Juni-33. Also see http://www.die-linke.de.
5. Perkins, John. *Confessions of an Economic Hitman,* San Francisco: Berrett-Koehler Publishers, Inc., 2004. http://resistir.info/livros/john_perkins_confessions_of_an_economic_hit_man.pdf
6. Rivero, Michael. *All Wars are Bankers Wars!* Accessed Dec. 25, 2015. http://whatreallyhappened.com/WRHARTICLES/allwarsarebankerwars.php#axzz3vLIQgixe
7. *http://www.cnn.com/2015/10/19/world/canadian-election/*
8. http://www.theatlantic.com/international/archive/2015/10/canada-justin-trudeau-election/411415/.
9. Sanders, Bernie. "Bernie Sanders: To Rein in Wall Street Fix the Fed," *New York Times,* Dec. 23, 2015. http://www.nytimes.com/2015/12/23/opinion/bernie-sanders-to-rein-in-wall-street-fix-the-fed.html?_r=0
10. Brown, Kailyn. "Bullet hole found at Sanders campaign HQ on day candidate was present," *Las Vegas Sun*, Published Jan. 8, 2016, updated Jan. 11, 2016. http://lasvegassun.com/news/2016/jan/08/bullet-hole-found-at-sanders-campaign-hq-on-day-ca/.
11. Chasmar, Jessica. "Former Secret Service agent: 'Don't be a sucker' for Bernie Sanders, *The Washington Times,* Jan. 4, 2016. http://www.washingtontimes.com/news/2016/jan/4/dan-bongino-former-secret-service-agent-dont-be-a-/.
12. Real Clear Politics. General Election: Trump vs. Sanders. http://www.realclearpolitics.com/epolls/2016/president/us/general_election_trump_vs_sanders-5565.html.
13. Politico. Polling Center. http://www.politico.com/polls/#.VppfnVMrJPM
14. Mckesson, Deray. "If you voted tomorrow, who would vote for to be the next President of the United States?" Twitter, Nov. 14, 2015. https://twitter.com/deray/status/665746154580258816?lang=en.
15. McKirdy, Euan. "Justin Trudeau, Liberals win clear majority in Canada elections," *CNN,* Oct. 20, 2015. http://www.cnn.com/2015/10/19/world/canadian-election/. Trudeau: Liberals won 184 seats to form the majority. (170 needed) Second youngest PM to come to power, but predicted for four decades earlier. http://www.theatlantic.com/international/archive/2015/10/canada-justin-trudeau-election/411415/.
16. BBC. "Labour leadership results in full," *BBC News,* Sept. 12, 2015. http://www.bbc.com/news/uk-politics-34221155 Jeremy Corbyn wants to cut tuition fees. So does the public (U.S. & U.K.).
17. RonPaul.com. "Audit the Federal Reserve," http://www.ronpaul.com/audit-the-federal-reserve-hr-1207/. (Ron Paul's beliefs are considered a mix of both Libertarian & Republican ideas. sanders.Senate.gov "The Fed Audit," July 21, 2011. http://www.sanders.senate.gov/newsroom/press-releases/the-fed-audit. Sanders considers himself a Democratic Socialist. Democrats voted against Rand Paul's (R-Ky) bill to audit the Fed in 2015. To balance the budget leftists want to raise taxes on the wealthy, while Libertarians want to reduce government spending and increase privatization schemes.
18. Fox Business. "Occupy Wall Street, Tea Party Movements Both Born of Bank Bailouts," FOXBusiness, Oct. 20, 2011. http://www.foxbusiness.com/markets/2011/10/19/occupy-wall-street-tea-party-born-bank-bailouts.html.

D1STRACT3D MA$$ES D1STRACT3D MA$$ES D1STRACT3D MA$$ES

BRIBES & BLACKMAIL

Politicians at a strip club.
Getting set up for their fall.
Captured on video.
So do what they say.
Or they'll release it all.

Shifting money in the treasury.
Between casino ATMs.
We need a racino.
Just ask the gaming commission.
Swore in.
Like the PED.
And PRC.
On a campaign contribution.

What's the solution?
#corruptnm #corruptkentucky
How'd we get so lucky,
To be able to buy our politicians?
Listen . . .

That's the sound of corruption.
How does government even
function,
With their bribes and blackmail?
Poker faced & pale.

Caught deep in their own lies.
The criminals wear ties.
Not tattoos.
Think about it.
It's true.

They are the gangsters

ENCRYPTED

Black box,
Data set.
Scrambled,
Coded.
Unintelligible.

Like background radiation.
Just static.
Extraterrestrial,
Secret messages,
Hidden signals.
Radiating.

Out of an inter-dimensional section,
Of the universe.
Splitting time into waveforms.
Beyond the dot com.

Underlying subliminal crypto,
Bitcoin track,
Trace.
PROMIS for tomorrow.
End line, terrorist, malfunction,
Malware.
Zero point,
Vulnerability.

Patchwork,
Mainframe.
Server.
Redirect.
Reconnect.
Scrambled & undetected.
Encrypted.

PRIVATE

Drones on the porch,
Telescopes pointed at my house,
Spy balloons and tapped phones,
Data transfer,
Sold to whoever.
Debt collector.
Straight out of the pen.

Private.
Lives shown on TV.
To millions.
Invasive.
In your smoke detector.
Smart thermostat.
Radio frequency.
Hack.

The brain,
Like Ghost in a Shell.
If it emits.
A signal.
They can.
They will.

Don't believe they can't.
Across broad spectrums.
Tapping your thoughts.
You are just an illusion.

You don't exist as one.
Privacy,
There's none.
We're all a holographic smeared
piece of code with the same info.

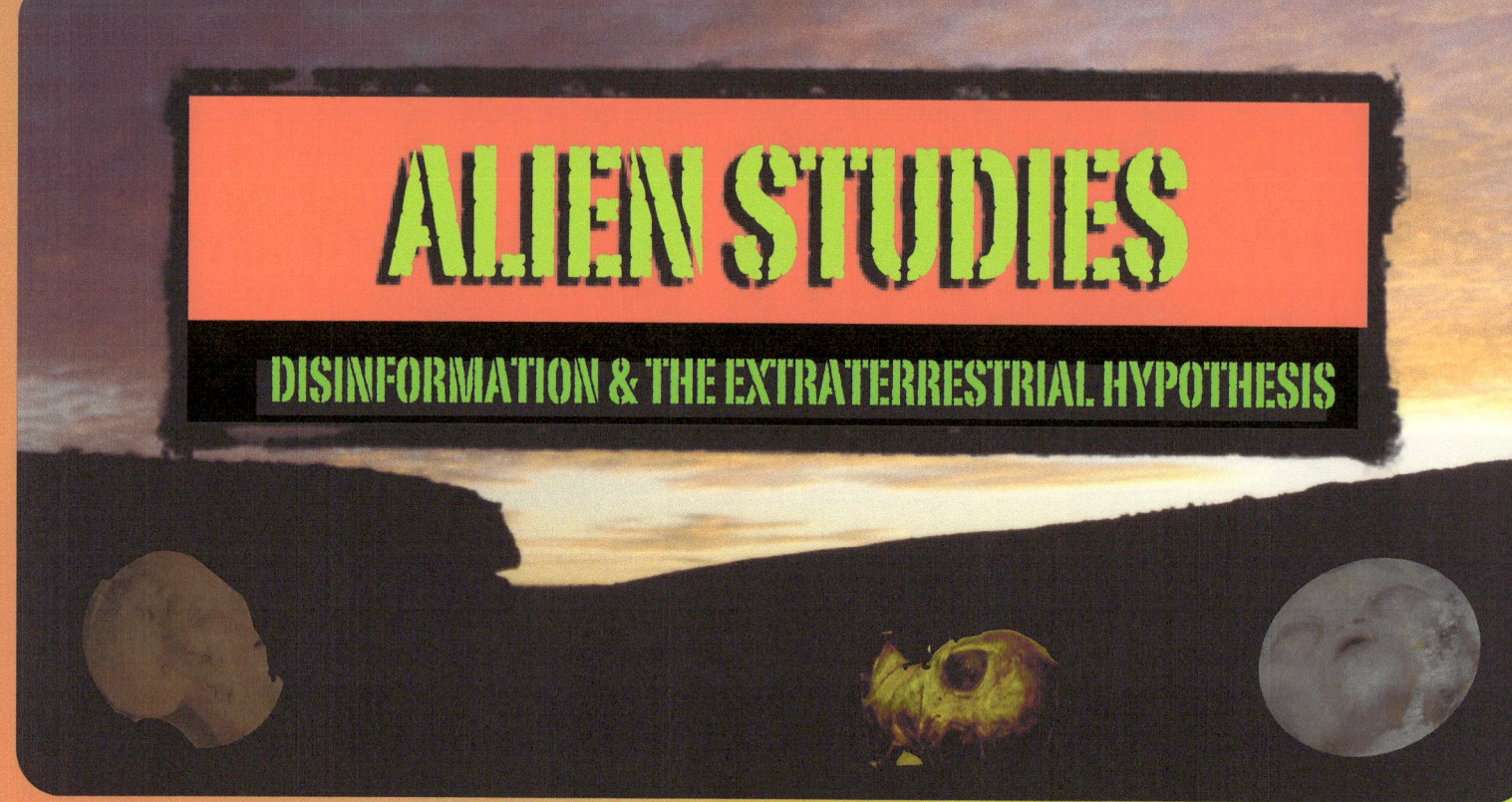

ALIEN STUDIES

DISINFORMATION & THE EXTRATERRESTRIAL HYPOTHESIS

By Scott Albright

I guess you can say I'm a believer in extraterrestrial life, and am not closed minded to any of the strange theories about the universe, multiverse, or whatever you want to call it. On the other hand, I don't have any real proof of there being anything out there except for what I've seen in documentaries, read in books, and experienced on my own. Proof, real proof, of extraterrestrials doesn't come easy. What I see with my own eyes could be an illusion, documentaries and books military disinformation, and other eye witness reports just a lively imagination or impaired mental state.

Proof, for me, is seeing the extraterrestrial lifeforms everyday. It's about NASA confirming it's existence with hard data and evidence. It's about corroboration, mass acceptance, and regular, every day sightings. So far, that does not exist, but what does exist as proof has led me to believe there is something very unusual going on. I don't just mean weird military operations, cover stories, and disinformation. I mean an actual logical explanation for things that perhaps humankind is not yet ready to confront. Things like teleportation and future transport systems. Things we think may now be possible, even though twenty or thirty years ago they were ideas only to be found in science fiction books. These were things that defied logic. They just couldn't be explained. And so it is with extraterrestrials as well, but perhaps it is our

I don't just mean weird military operations, cover stories, and disinformation. I mean an actual logical explanation for things that perhaps humankind is not yet ready to confront.

understanding of logic itself that may help us to understand what is going on just a little better.

What we have, on the one hand, is a purely scientific and logical approach to searching the skies for signs of life via radio telescopes, satellites, robotic spacecraft, and other technologies and instruments. It's serious, scientific, and has even brought indirect evidence of the possibility of some other type of lifeforms out there in the universe. The masses have accepted this as a serious study, but still it has brought little in the way of understanding what is going on right here on Earth. On the other (not-so-scientific) hand, there is an abundance of what many would call amateur studies of abductions, sightings, and other direct contacts with extraterrestrial beings. These latter studies tend to be dismissed by the mainstream as illogical quasi-science, metaphysics, or trippy-hippy new age nonsense. But not all of it is. Leslie Kean's book *UFOs: Generals, Pilots, And Government Officials Go On The Record* (see book review on page 62) provides eye witness accounts of high ranking military officials' dealings with the UFO and extraterrestrial phenomenon. The book is serious in it's approach to understanding unexplainable aerial phenomenon witnessed by pilots and military officials, all the while arguing in a logical and consistent manner as to why we should take theories of extraterrestrial visitation to this planet seriously. Kean points out how multiple witnesses refused to take even their own sightings of an unexplainable ev-

-ent seriously. Kean says witnesses to a hovering saucer-like craft over the United Airlines terminal at Chicago O'Hare was debunked as a strange weather event even though the explanation for the event was not even a possibility given the weather conditions at the time, yet everyone, even the witnesses, would go along with the story so as not to be ridiculed for telling others what they saw. Kean points out how this 'look the other way' approach to understanding strange aerial phenomenon can be dangerous to public safety and national security.

Perhaps national security is precisely the reason why the U.S. government has not whole-heartedly welcomed the extraterrestrial hypothesis. Books like Greg Bishop's *Project Beta* and Ion Mihai Pacepa's *Disinformation* give us a basic understanding of why the government might want to use disinformation to deceive the public about such phenomenon in the name of national security. If perhaps the U.S. government let the public know they were serious about investigating UFO sightings and extraterrestrial theories, than some major vulnerabilities to air traffic safety and national security may very well be exposed and taken advantage of by adversaries. Downplaying the sightings makes the U.S. government appear as though there are no issues at hand and that everything is under control, when perhaps everything is not. Things that cannot be explained make adversaries more curious and provide new ways to exploit vulnerabilities in air defense and tracking systems while also giving up valuable information about emergency response times, new technologies, social reactions, personnel, hierarchical command structures, and emergency priority management. These are just a few of the reasons why the U.S. government would want to feed the masses disinformation about extraterrestrials and UFO technologies, but perhaps the most obvious is that of advanced weapons and military equipment research and development.

Besides the obvious need to coverup military weapons programs, the U.S. government would also want to misdirect and confuse the public about real extraterrestrial craft for similar reasons. If a UFO really did crash on Earth than there is no doubt military officials from all over the planet would be interested in learning how to use the technologies for their own countries. So, the U.S. government probably does take UFO sightings seriously for these reasons, and there probably are officials who are well versed in the extraterrestrial hypothesis and who do respond to unexplained aerial phenomenon as potential national security threats, but these officials are behind the scenes. They cannot be the public face of the U.S. government's investigation into matters of extraterrestrials and flying saucers. No, these officials must protect what they know with walls of lies and constant flows of disinformation to confuse and distract the masses. But how do we find these officials? And what can they tell us that we don't already know?

As long as we are at war and in a constant state of violent conflict I don't think the U.S. government will ever tell us, or publicly take the extraterrestrial hypothesis seriously, as there is too much at stake for the full truth to be told out in the open. I do think though that with the continued development of the communication devices we already have, it will one day be impossible to keep all the evidence out of sight. Already, one can cruise the internet and find millions of videos and photos of UFO sightings and alien encounters. Photo and video experts have analyzed tons of these recordings and have found many to be unexplainable. On a worldwide scale it's hard to say how much evidence there already is from eyewitnesses who have documented their sightings and experiences, but one can say there is enough to say we definitely have *some* evidence of extraterrestrial craft visiting planet Earth. Is the evidence damning? Not really, but it's at least as good as the "evidence" we're presented when governments use the media to smear their opposition in order to justify going to war against them. But that's a different story entirely. Or is it?

There are plenty of news stories and books out there which point out how governments use Hollywood movies like Star Wars to plant ideas into people's minds about extraterrestrials, future technologies, and space conflicts for the purpose of getting them used to such possibilities in the real world. The toy stores are flooded with Star Wars junk and knickknacks, while the media hype each new movie release like it's the most amazing thing in the world. Children growing up playing with toy lasers and ray guns will have no problem as adults with governments spending trillions of dollars on black budget space weapons programs, as their minds will have already accepted the need for such things after being brainwashed by the media for so long. And when a Russian fighter jet is shot down or a satellite blasted out of orbit people will think of it as normal, as though the "foreign threat" is no different than a (dehumanized) evil alien army that must be eliminated through the development and use of more high tech weapons and military technologies. Ideas about the need for such weapons brought forth through movies and pop culture are reinforced by the mainstream news media which sanitize the images of war for their viewers, making the violence all the more acceptable for those sitting in the comfort of their homes.

But that's not the end of the psychological techniques the government uses to change the ment-

-al perspective of the masses. Disinformation about extraterrestrials and alien craft allows the government to hide secret weapons programs, while also being able to cover up threats to national security by spreading rumors about "UFO" crash sites to the media which were really secret military "weather" (i.e. reconnaissance) balloons. Spreading rumors about UFOs and aliens helps to create confusion and misdirection, all the while helping to keep the truth out of the hands of snoopy reporters and foreign spies. But that doesn't mean everything out there is disinformative, nor does it mean there aren't real people working for the government which take the threat of extraterrestrial & unexplained aerial phenomenon just as seriously as the threat of foreign aircraft flying in restricted air space. Such threats have to be taken seriously as they are both possibilities which the government has to prepare for.

Preparing for incursions into national air space by the type of advanced technologies extraterrestrials may have could be even more advantageous to the military than just preparing for incursions by aircraft we already know about. Defense strategists no doubt incorporate some of these types of potential incursions into their war games and response plans. There is no reason the military wouldn't scramble a jet to confront an unknown advanced type of aircraft over an identifiable one, however there are many reasons such plans and actual events would be kept secret from the public, so knowing what's real and what isn't becomes all the more difficult to discern.

Photo of newspaper at Roswell UFO Museum

It is my belief that this is precisely why the U.S. government *should* take the extraterrestrial hypothesis more seriously - because it *is* a national security issue. The walls of lies and disinformation sow distrust and doubt into the minds of the masses and prevents witnesses from coming forward with their stories. By being more welcoming and open to the idea of extraterrestrial craft on Earth, than perhaps more people would be willing to report what they have seen - strange weather phenomenon, foreign craft, or even direct contact with beings from other planets. The more information the government collects about these sightings and the more it welcomes them and takes them seriously, the more intelligence they will be able to gather in order to enhance national security. To me, it's logical, but then again some accounts of these extraterrestrial technologies defy all logic anyway, so perhaps taking the logical approach isn't the best way about it. So

perhaps things that defy logic shouldn't be logically explained. If we don't understand it, applying our own reasoning to the phenomenon will only deduce our observations down to the level of what we *can* understand.

Taking a more illogical approach, and accepting all accounts of sightings and communications with extraterrestrial beings as being just as possible as anything else, will open up new avenues of study that would otherwise be ignored. When we deny the reality of one's observations, no matter who that person is, we deny ourselves access to a reality that has the potential to lead us along a more diverse pathway. A mentally ill person's observations of an alien craft shouldn't be dismissed simply because they have a different psychological approach to reality than you or I. Children, too, should be taken seriously, perhaps *because* the imagination of a child is so powerful. Children have the potential to bring to life ingenious ideas many adults could never think up. And what we "bring to life" has absolutely everything to do with the extraterrestrial hypothesis, because if we deny it as a possibility than it will remain but just a hypothesis, and a dead one at that.

According to Wikipdia, the extraterrestrial hypothesis (ETH) "proposes that some unidentified flying objects (UFOs) are best explained as being physical spacecraft occupied by extraterrestrial life or non-human aliens from other planets visiting Earth. As yet, no evidence exists to support this hypothesis." But often times the evidence we do have suggests nothing less. But because of the disinfo, it seems that nobody will ever know if the extraterrestrial hypothesis is correct. Yes, disinformation can cover certain things up, but it can also leave more unexplained than it does explained, making one wonder if there isn't something more out there than just secret weapons research programs. And if all the sightings are nothing but just secret weapons programs, than the government needs to do a better job trying to deceive the people, as often times their explanation is more illogical and improbable than the possibility of a visitor from another planet, however am personally against using disinformation for any reason and believe the government should be more transparent in it's testing of new weapons systems, while also taking the extraterrestrial hypothesis seriously. Spreading disinfo not only sows distrust in the public, but it also hinders serious investigations and can drive researchers mad.

Greg Bishop's book *Project Beta* explains how in 1980 a guard at Kirtland Air Force Base (KAFB) reported seeing a glowing craft crash to the ground and then take back off after he approached it while standing guard near a nuclear weapons storage area. A few months later all the radar went out throughout Albuquerque unexplainably. The lead character in Bishop's book, Paul Bennewitz, is a scientist living near the base at the time who has sightings of his own and reports his findings to the Air Force. Bennewitz is fed disinformation to prevent him from learning more, with Russian spooks apparently also on the hunt for whatever was going on at KAFB. Readers learn that something took place near Coyote Canyon, a place on base where nukes are rumored to be stored and where local police have been trained alongside military personnel and officials from the Department of Energy, supposedly with machine-guns and other high powered weapons. Bishop speculates the craft sightings were related to unmanned aerial vehicle (UAV) experiments or the nearby StarFire observatory's lasers. He says the Defense Intelligence Agency and the National Security Agency may have also been involved in whatever was going on there at the time. Whatever it was that was there, it was important enough for Bennowitz to be lied to by military officials for investigating the matter, enough to make him go crazy and be institutionalized, Bishop tells us.

Looking down from the Sandia mountains one can see there is a huge canyon alongside the edge of the base near the bottom of the mountains where Coyote Canyon is located. The canyon seems to extend far up into the mountains, and it is said that the base borders some of the bike paths and trails near Tunnel Canyon where people have said to have been apprehended by military personnel for going too far off the trails. Bishop's speculations about UAVs and laser facilities may be accurate, yet we are still left without a real explanation as to what the guard near Coyote Canyon had seen or what Bennewitz was looking at glowing in the night sky above KAFB. It took an independent researcher just to point out the lies that were told, yet he still couldn't get us the truth, leaving his readers only knowing who not to believe, not what to believe.

One of the main themes throughout all the UFOology is the amount of increased sightings at or near nuclear facilities. Of course the first possibility that comes to mind is foreign spies or military operations, but what's baffling about many of the sightings is that no one has been able to really explain them in a comprehensible way, particularly those on military installations. We should take this seriously because they should be explainable. If the eye witnesses and lead investigators of the various military related sightings near nuclear facilities or military bases can't explain what was seen, than it is absolutely fair to consider the possibility of something coming from outside of Earth, and that should most definitely be taken seriously by our public officials. Leaving no explanation and not taking the extraterrestrial hypothesis seriously makes it appear as though there is something to hide or that military officials are ashamed of the vulnerabilities in their security. Either way, leaving the public wondering does not help the situation further. Maybe, in this day and age of human and robotic space travel, we just might want to consider the possibility that another species is doing the same thing as us, perhaps with much greater technologies than our own. It might be wise to prepare for such a thing anyway, just in case.

But until we stop denying the possibility and ridiculing eye witnesses of alien sightings than we won't be able to research the topic seriously. If we can't even accept it as a possibility, much less a reality, than it cannot be in the minds' of the masses as such, for we would just deny it's existence anyway. Alien visitors to this planet is too much of an impossibility in the minds of most people that it will remain that way for some time - impossible. But if we take it seriously, if more of us really begin to research the full picture of the extraterrestrial hypothesis, we might just be able to comprehend the possibilities, and we might even find what we're looking for. But many of us choose to accept only one of the many possibilities there are to our reality, and that is okay too. We must make life coherent, and we must choose logical, probable paths in order to manifest our own individual desired realities. And of course the media, alongside the social cues of the day, help to shape these individual realities which are tied together collectively, but still, many realities are far different than others. And it seems as though reality can be hardwired, as though the individual's neural pathways have been engraved permanently into one route within the mind's conscious self. There is no possible new reality along pathways of this sort, even if the persons have witnessed unexplainable events themselves. Even if they know what they experienced can not be logically explained.

But many don't accept what the U.S. government proposes to the masses as a "logical explanation," many times because their explanations aren't logical at all. Often times the extraterrestrial hypothesis seems much more logical, and plausible, than the explanations the U.S. government gives us, so many continue to research these Earth-based sightings very seriously, whether the U.S. government is publicly on board or not. Now that more people ha-

-ve access to more recording devices and faster communication than ever before, it has become even easier for those who do take extraterrestrial visitations seriously to share their intelligence with each other. Rather than just letting the government and mainstream media handle it all, these new UFO and alienologists are blazing the way for future research regarding this phenomenon. They will probably be the first to have confirmed public contact with extraterrestrials while everyone else laughs because they don't take the possibility seriously. I will continue to take the possibility seriously, but until I meet one of these extraterrestrials it will still only be a possibility - a possibility I will continue to keep my mind open to.

References

1. Reichbach, Matthew. "Astronaut from NM says aliens stopped nuclear wars," *The NM Political Report,* Aug. 18, 2015. http://nmpoliticalreport.com/10548/astronaut-from-nm-says-aliens-stopped-nuclear-wars/.

2. Kean, Leslie. *UFOs: Generals, Pilots, And Government Officials Go On The Record (Brazillian comments on nukes and national security).* Three Rivers Press, Aug. 2, 2011.

3. Bishop, Greg. *Project Beta The Story of Paul Bennewitz, National Security, and the Modern UFO Myt*h, Gallery Books, Feb. 8, 2005.

4. UPARS. "Greg Bishop (09-21-06) PROJECT BETA: How the U.S. Government Created an Alien Invasion, *YouTube*, Published Feb. 11, 2015. shttps://www.youtube.com/watch?v=u7MbZfOZcO8

5. "The Maelstrom Air Fore Base UFO/Missile Incident (Nuclear missiles shutdown during UFO encounter). *UFO Evidence, Scientific Study of of the UFO Phenomenon and the Search for Extraterrestrial Life,* http://www.ufoevidence.org/cases/case1017.htm.

6. Walia, Arjun. "Why Are UFOs Shutting Down Our Nuclear Missiles?" *Collective Evolution,* Nov. 10, 2014. http://www.collective-evolution.com/2014/11/10/why-are-ufos-shutting-down-our-nuclear-missiles/.

7. UFOs and Nukes. "About UFOs and Nuclear Weapons," http://www.ufohastings.com/

8. Rojas, Alejandro. "UFO Buzzed French NuclearPower Plant Says Director," *Huffington Post,* Jan. 28, 2015. http://www.huffingtonpost.com/alejandro-rojas/ufo-buzzed-french-nuclear_b_6558798.html.

9. The Rendlesham Forest Incident - Official Website, http://www.therendleshamforestincident.com/.

10. Hilkevitch, Jon. "In the sky! A bird? A plane? A . . . UFO? *Chicago Tribune,* Jan. 4, 2007. http://articles.chicagotribune.com/2007-01-01/travel/chi-0701010141jan01_1_craig-burzych-controllers-in-o-hare-tower-united-plane.

DISTRACTION!

Donald Trump,
Edward Bernays
WMDs, Libya, Email,
Qaddafi.
Drop me.
Off at MCRD,
I'm off to fight the battle,
The war.

Special info ops . . .

. . . Drops, bombs on to the people,
Out in never nowhere.

Losers are everywhere.
Except those.
In their high rise.
Trying to get us to divide.

Another piece of the pie.

HELICOPTER

Buzzing my house at 6 a.m.
Noise ordinance violation!
Adrenalin rushing.
PTSD syndrome.

Black ops.
In the middle of the night.
Helicopter.
Comin' in for a landing.

They rush out.
DIA, black ninjas in,
Invisible Iron Man suits.
Don't see the infrared light they shoot.

Helicopter.
Comin' in for a landing.
Please don't say it's crashing.
Helicopter.
Givin' me bad dreams at night.

The buzzing rotor blades.
Through the night they slice.
Not so silent tonight.
Chopping up the air.

Helicopter.
For the people below you don't care.
Gun 'em down.
Blast 'em up!
Helicopter man don't give a fuck.

But don't come crashing down!
You might hurt us below.
From flying debris.
Please.
Helicopter.
Just go away.

TIMELESS CAMOUFLAGE

streaking across
the screen
matrix
dream

reality
or is it?
What just happened?
imaginary

dust from a fairy
FREAKY
dEaTh!
but no one in sight

cosmic smear
electronic crush
ELIMINATE SURVEILLANCE!
When time stops.
For a stop watch.

It's a false illusion on our clocks
the strangest manifestation
of reality ever
to exist
in the entire multiverse.

Erasing all memory,
and eViDeNcE
of it ever happening.
blink your eyes
and it's forgotten
Never seen.

Must've been a dream.
The greatest hoax.
to EVER be pulled!
A fake false flag,
wrapped in timeless camouflage.

MANIFESTING REALITY: Information to Action

By Scott Albright

To dream up one's own reality is going against the nature of God to some. According to many religions, we are here as open vassals to God in which we provide Him our bodies to help manifest the reality He finds most suited for us. Our leaders are chosen by God through some form of Manifest Destiny or Mandate of Heaven in order to provide us with the guidance we need to create our collective reality. To believe it to be any other way would be Satanic, or at least politically unacceptable, and even punishable by death in countries like Saudi Arabia or China. Or so it seems that's the message I have received through readings of various scriptures and literature passed on and stored on one side of the library.

But on the other side there are books like *The Secret* which tells us how the law of attraction can be used by individuals as a means of manifesting their own realities. Individual free will and self autonomy is encouraged and the imagination pointed to as a guiding post for creating future pathways. This is the opposite of giving ourselves up to some higher being, entity, faction, cult, or secret society. This is about control and self determination - individual creation, self guidance, and free will. But there is a catch to this. The more independent we become, the more free will we have - the more controlled and orderly things will be. The more we plan and script our own futures outside of the random external influences we would normally find in our lives, the more our lives become deterministic. Through self creation we gain more free will, but we also lose some by our elimination of chance and randomness. So before attempting to write our futures out in long hand, it's important to recognize these two opposing, yet complementary factors. Determinism and free will are both inevitable natural consequences of the universe's evolution, so we must accept that we cannot control everything, and that not everything can control us.

That being said, there is a way to regulate the external influences in a way which positively contributes to our own desired future outcomes. Key to this is knowledge and information. The information we consume and the knowledge we hold influences the way we think, and in turn changes the type of actions we take. Luckily we have vast amounts of information at our fingertips to pick and choose from, so we no longer have to submit our minds to the force fed information of those who have an interest in controlling what we think and how we behave. Of course we don't always know the details about all the information we decide to consume beforehand, so there will be surprises and some force fed information we may need to toss aside, but compared to when there was no internet, we are at an advantage as to the variety of information that is available for our consumption.

Choosing the type of information we decide to consume is not an easy task, but one can give themselves some basic guidelines. We must ask, what is it that we truly want for ourselves in the future? What do we want for our children, and what is the best type of reality to manifest not just for one self, but for the world at large? It's natural for humans to have selfish desires that are not always healthy for one self or the people around them, so there are moral and ethical questions one must wade through before deciding what one truly wants to manifest as their reality. After coming to terms with these issues, one can then decide which types of information they want to consume.

For me, there are some basic needs I have to satisfy. First off is money - money for student loans, rent, utilities, retirement, investments in children, and savings is needed for the well being of my family and their overall mental and physical health. Therefore, I need information about how to make money to satisfy all these different needs. So what I do is seek out this information on the internet, follow social media accounts which provide information about how to satisfy these financial needs, and look for books at the library which can give me the knowledge I need to reach my goals. Finding the most relevant and reliable sources is another big task, but each individual is different, so the information they consume will also be different, however there are certain types of information which can be considered standards for comparison or relational purposes, as for our manifested realities to be considered true to others we must have some standard for all to relate to. Encyclopedias, dictionaries, first hand sources, and official historical records are some examples of the collective informational standards we can use to refer to to satisfy this end.

Wading through all the information can be time consuming, especially when trying to meet other needs as well, such as health, happiness, peace, etc. There are literally millions of websites which provide information about these topics, many of them extremely useful and practical, however too much information can slow one down in their ultimate goal of creating their realities, so it is important to have specific goals which require a limited, specific type of information, and to set timelines on when you want to reach these goals, and only consume the amount of information needed to meet the original goal one set out to do.

Some goals are much easier to meet, but often times it's because those are the goals one wants to meet the most. For example, one of my goals is to be more healthy, so I decided to start playing soccer again to do this. I love soccer so it's not a difficult goal for me to achieve even with having to manage a somewhat hectic and non-routine schedule as a single dad raising three kids. But when you want something bad enough, you find a way to do it. The internet made this goal achievable much quicker than I had anticipated. After browsing and searching through the different league websites I finally found what I was really looking for - Saturday co-ed pick up games at UNM. Perfect! The next step was going from information consumption to action. All I had to do was sign up with the online Meet-Up group, RSVP, and head down to the field at 10 am. Easy. Although I haven't been able to make every game, I have been able to make Saturday morning soccer a more regular part of my life for a few months now. This has been the easiest case of information to action reality manifestation for me to date, but not all goals are as easy to manifest into reality.

I'm still working on reaching specific financial goals that I have been unable to meet for years no matter what information I use as a way to take action. I have found though that perseverance, patience, and a positive mind are helpful in reaching this goal. For all my life I have been fed this idea that money is the root of an evil greed that is blinding us from our moral and social responsibilities. I have been led to believe that money is communal - that what goes around comes around - and that sharing and giving are signs of good character, while receiving and taking are signs of greed and selfishness. Time sheets, time clocks, and administrative or managerial policies have conditioned me to believe that my time and energy is less valuable than others. I am consumed with this overwhelming feeling of guilt if I take more than I am led to believe I deserve. This conditioning and way of thinking is due to the type of information I've consumed and been force fed by others, and it is deeply rooted into my neural pathways and difficult to change simply by consuming new types of information that refute these ways of thinking. Such ways of thinking are some of the major roadblocks I've encountered while trying to reach my financial goals, yet those roadblocks can be rammed through or bypassed with enough persistence and determination, no matter what one's circumstances are. Yes, you may be trapped in the ghetto, living in a drought prone region of the world, or mentally or physically handicapped, but there are ways around these hurdles, and information & knowledge is still the key.

The secret, the real secret, to manifesting one's desired reality is knowing what one really wants. Yes, I want money to help me meet my financial goals, but I need to be more specific than this. I need to know how and why I want to bring this money into reality. I've found that working for others, especially when it comes to writing, is very difficult for me. Often times I simply don't want to work for anyone else because I don't want to write what they want me to write. Manual labor, on the other hand, is much easier for me to do just by obeying commands and following orders, partially because the Marine Corps ingrained that into me, but also because I often want to just be told what to do - I find it easier. For me, manual labor can be refreshing because I don't have to think much about what I'm doing - because I'm an open vassal to those in charge. It's blissful at times, but it is because I am not thinking, because there is a lack of intellect-

-ual challenge in my work, that I stop enjoying manual labor. For me, being told what to do every step of the way (especially by overly-critical bosses) is simply not satisfying. If I don't enjoy it, if I don't want to do it, it's going to be much more difficult for me to be motivated to climb through the ranks or up that corporate ladder.

So this is where I've become stuck, because the reality is that to make money you have to be an agent at some point. In principal-agent theory one can flip their roles in many different settings, but when it comes to exchanging money, the one receiving the cash is almost always the agent. Now my grandfather, who passed away not long ago, told me that what I need to do is figure out a way to pay myself, so that I can be both the principal and the agent, but the only way I've come up with to do that is to start my own business, which when looking at the current economic landscape seems like a pretty bad idea. But I think the reward might be worth it in the end.

What I'll need is your help though. Readers of *Distracted Masses* have to give me a boost in this financial manifestation. The goal: Turn *Distracted Masses* into a business - a real business. The details will be laid out in a business plan, and courses taken in order to obtain the knowledge needed for success, but in the end it will be up to those reading the works herein that will make it all become a reality, and your feedback is essential. It isn't just about how you can help me to pay myself, but also how I, the writer, can help you to pay yourself. How can we collectively manifest the realities we want together? In order to become financially successful as a business there is nothing more important than satisfying the needs of those the business serves, and in this case it is both the readers and the writers of this publication. More of how we can work together to manifest our desired realities will come in later issues, but first let me get to why I believe self-creating our future realities is not only possible, but very necessary for the future of our species.

Using information to take the actions necessary to manifest one's desired reality is easy to understand. There is even an Albuquerque-area "Law of Attraction" Meet-Up group one can go to to learn more about how all this works, something I may consider doing. On the group's Meet-Up page it says that one skeptical member was able to manifest a trip to Hawaii within one month, while another member "got over 17 thousand dollars by a series of miraculous events." But one does not have

to read *The Secret* or go to one of these law of attraction groups to see the miracles of self-creation, and the usefulness of information, knowledge, and technology in making it all work.

The Meet-Up website provides some of the best evidence for proving that self-creation and the law of attraction works. All you have to do is simply know what you are attracted to, find a group interested in the same thing, join up, and voila - presto-bingo reality creation manifestation. Put it this way - the Albuquerque Active & Looking for Fun group started as just one person, and now boasts over 1,400 members. According to the site, the organizer asked himself, "What is the most efficient and quickest way in which to meet people in my new city while having fun at the same time?" Meet-Up was clearly his answer, and apparently a good choice. Now others who also want to have fun around Albuquerque can join in and suggest ways in which they can all collectively create their fun realities by requesting the type of events the group will host or participate in.

But the larger reality, the one outside of these little social groups, is the reality that really needs to be collectively manifested in new ways. Small groups and factions have always been able to

Falcon1

T-Shirt

create their own little realities, and have even shaped the realities outside of their little groups, but as human beings we are more than just a bunch of groups with different desires and needs. Some of our basic desires and needs are the same, no matter which group one self-identifies with. Most humans do have a desire to stay alive, and most humans do have a desire to live in a peaceful state. Most humans want to be loved and want to be healthy and happy. Of course what makes one person happy can make another miserable, but still, there is a commonality in our desire to be happy.

In Buddhism this desire is frowned upon. Individual self satisfaction is at the root of our suffering. To desire anything is to cause more suffering. In the Yoga Sutras of Patanjali it is said that one must even give up the desire for desirelessness. Once we give up this desire and the sense of need to satisfy one's self wants, then we become a part of a larger reality where we are no longer an individual, but one with the whole. Again, we must give ourselves up to some outside force and become a vassal of change, rather than the vassal which creates the change. Again, we see how free will and determinism become mishmashed into some larger reality. So we must stop and ask if having a lack of desire is truly the best way to manifest this reality of non-suffering. I personally think it is self-defeating, as if we lose all desire - desire to procreate, to eat or drink, or to survive - than we will all die. Only those who were thirsty, hungry, and horny would survive, but I could be wrong.

Indeed, I believe some form of spiritual journey is necessary for one to be able to help collectively manifest a new reality for future generations, but I'm not sure giving all of my "self" up to some higher being or spiritual force is necessary. In fact, I think it could be very dangerous if that spiritual force is being guided by another individual or group of individuals' selfish desires. Too many times have young men and women given themselves up to some higher force - be that God, the Marine Corps, the state, or some secret cult - only to find out they were only being used to achieve someone's else's objectives, not the shared goals and dreams they had publicly stated they sought to reach. I even met a Marine Corps infantry instructor who told me the Marine Corps was his religion, the commandant his god. He'd given his soul to the Corps, not out of any selfish desire of his own, but in order to carry out the mission of God through killing and combat. No, I have to reject this type of reality manifestation. As a collective, the Marines can manifest their own desired realities, but at what cost and for whose benefit?

No, I think I'd rather rely on my own mind to find the information I need to create the reality I want - the reality I hope will help others, no matter what group they self-identify with. Of course the military and police also use information to action as a way of manifesting realities that are more beneficial to the masses. Information collected from intelligence units can help to prevent crimes and atrocities, and does in fact alter the reality of the masses, but because access to this information is unavailable to most, because transparency has yet to be the norm, the reality they manifest will be unknown to us beforehand, and hence cannot be a part of any type of collective manifestation of reality. But access to information is still key for the rest of us, whether it be classified state secrets, or ancient spiritual texts not made available to the public. The more information we have, the more we can independently and discriminatively discern between what information we need and don't need to build the reality we all desire.

You might say you don't have the time and are too busy to even care if you have access to this information. You might say you don't mind carrying out the will of God, or Allah, or Buddha, or the Commandant. And you might say you don't mind being an open vassal to your corporate slavemaster, ripping up the land and exploiting the Earth in the name of God's chosen economic system. And that's your choice. You may feel like you don't have a choice, but you know you do, and it's fine if the choice you decide creates more fragmented and opposing realities, but one day we may not have a choice anymore and will have to work together to create our reality as human beings, and not just our little self-identifying groups. One day we may all have to identify as human beings, as one species, just in order to survive.

Until then I'm going to do my best to prevent myself from becoming an open vassal for others to create their desired realities through. I will continue to seek more information and to share that information with as many people as possible so that we can all independently, yet collectively, decide which information we need most to better manifest a reality that is beneficial to all. We must start with ourselves, and create the realities that are best for each individual, and then move on tho the larger reality. In a way we give our "self" up just a bit when we receive from and share information with others. In a way, we become more of a whole, particularly when the same information is used to create large-scale realities for the masses, yet we still remain a "self". So let's seek out the information we need to manifest this reality. Or just sit idly by and let others create it for you. The choice is yours.

References/Further Reading

1. Patrick. "The 7 Huna Principles of Life 3. MAKIA," *Unwrap Your Mind,* http://www.unwrapyourmind.com/the-7-huna-principles-of-life-%E2%80%93-3-makia/.
2. Byrne, Rhonda. *The Secret,* New York: Atria Books, 2006. https://docs.google.com/file/d/0ByqvewEmgwYXZkxXSEM0bENvWjQ/edit.
3. Meet-Up. "Albuquerque Soccer Pickup," founded Apr. 3, 2015. http://www.meetup.com/ABQPickup/.
4. Meet-Up. "The Albuquerque Law of Attraction Group," founded Jan. 6, 2009. http://www.meetup.com/albuquerquelawofattraction/.
5. Meet-Up. "Active & Looking for Fun," founded Jul. 7, 2009. http://www.meetup.com/Active-and-Looking-for-Fun/.
6. Sanchez, Yoanni. "From Information to Action: Yoani Sanchez Acceptance Speech for Knight International Journalism Award, *The Global Post,* Nov. 12, 2015. http://www.huffingtonpost.com/yoani-sanchez/from-information-to-actio_b_8546858.html.
7. Carl-Jung.net. "What is Synchronicity?" http://www.carl-jung.net/synchronicity.html.
8. Bahm, Archie J. *Yoga Union with the Ultimate: A new version of the ancient Yoga Sutras of Patanjali,* New York: Frederick Ungar Publishing Co. 1961.
9. Herr, Eva. *Consciousness and the New Super Science of Quantum Mechanics,* Faber, Virginia: Rainbow Ridge Books, 2012.

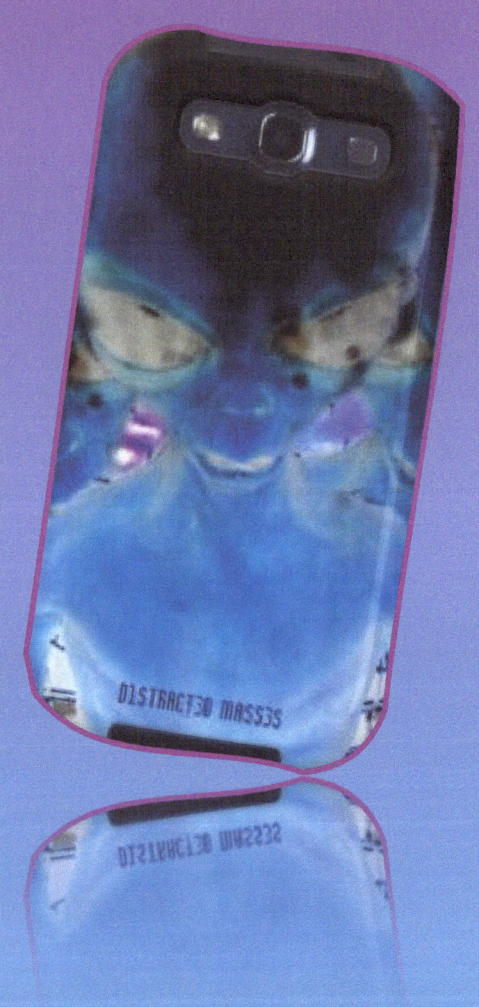

DISTRACT3D ALIENS

Support The Mission!

Buy cool stuff at: http://www.zazzle.com/scajax
And: http://www.zazzle.com/distractedmasses.

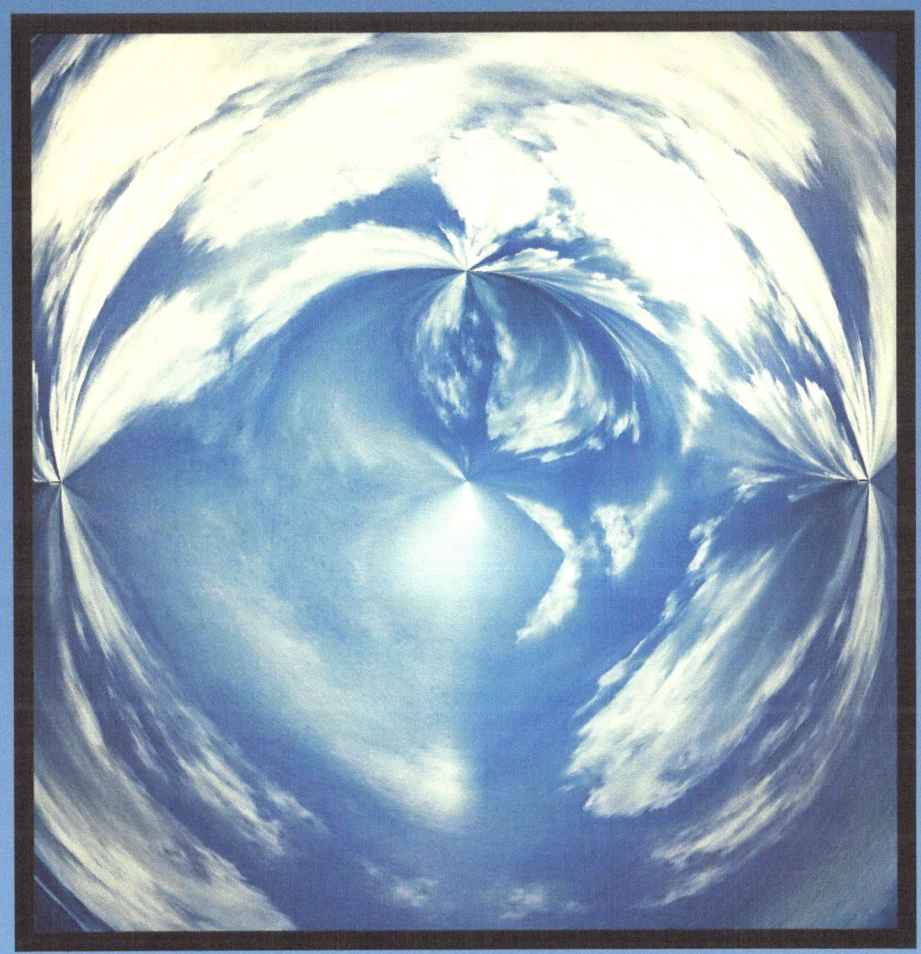

Purchases made from the Zazzle store help to keep writers at Distracted Masses happy, focused, and stress free.

In order to continue producing quality content Distracted Masses needs your help. Donations can be made via PayPal by transferring funds to distractedmasses1@gmail.com . The more donations and financial incentive you provide, the more time Distracted Masses can spend conducting interviews, researching, writing, and getting the content out to you.

Distracted Masses is now accepting sponsored articles ideas.
If there is an article you want us to write, send your bid and article idea to distractedmasses1@gmail.com. We look forward to your support!

CALL FOR MEDIA!

Do have a paper, essay, or article, about concentration, distraction, disinformation, media analysis, or political communication that you want to see published in *Distracted Masses*? If so, we want to see what you have. Are you an independent media outlet looking to get your articles published on other sites? We can help. *Distracted Masses* is open to receiving articles, book reviews, poetry, photographs, art, and video to display online and in our upcoming issues. In exchange, *Distracted Masses* will provide you with your own advertising space as well as the freedom to publish any of *Distracted Masses'* work on your own website or publication. We use a commercial creative commons license which allows content in our publication and on our website to be republished and altered by others for profit. We are utilizing the share economy to get our work out to as many people as possible, while allowing others to benefit from our work. The idea is that if more people share their work across the different alternative media outlets, the more each writer will be acknowledged, helping to create name recognition while also bringing in new readers and increasing product and/or service sales for each content creator.

We know that if your work gets published in *Distracted Masses* you will be proud to show it off to friends, helping to drive traffic and bring in new potential long term customers to our publication & website. And when our work is published on your site, we do the same. We tell our friends, help to drive traffic to your site, and ultimately increase revenue for your writers and content creators. Most media outlets are in competition with each other, trying to steal advertisers and subscribers from one another. It's a zero sum game, and *Distracted Masses* doesn't believe in this approach. We believe in creating win-win situations, and think the share economy is the way to make it happen. We will be developing a business plan over the next several months to help improve our ability to make the share economy work for us and our supporters. Until then, we will utilize the plan we've been going off so far - and that's just to write. Do what we can, when we can, with what we got. The creator of *Distracted Masses*, Scott Albright, is a single dad raising three kids on his own while struggling with PTSD, so what is being done is quite amazing when considering the little amount of time and financial support Scott has received thus far. So please, take the time to send an article, a video, or piece of artwork to distractedmasses1@gmail.com and help to get the share economy rolling. Your writing is a commodity that has great value. Together we can amplify the value of that commodity.

Submitted articles should be no more than 2,000 words, using 12 point New Times Roman font, with Chicago style citations and a full list of references, not to be included in the word count. Send all submissions to distractedmasses1@gmail.com with the word SUBMISSION in the subject line. Distracted Masses is always interested in hearing your thoughts on how we can improve. Please send all suggestions, questions, or ideas to the above email. Thanks for your support!

#TWITTERMANIA: FRAMING THE MSM'S AGENDA

By Scott Albright

Where do you get your news? Where does the news get its news? Being a Twitter maniac myself I've come to notice that the news is often two or three days behind what Twitter users have been discussing. Live shots, pictures, and descriptions of events from the wide variety of users allows for instantaneous information to flow from an abundance of diverse sources. The news simply can't keep up, but they are paying attention. And that's what's interesting.

Scores of news sites run Twitter feeds below their news articles, often times with the tweets filling up more space than the article itself. I have no problem with this as Twitter is a public space and if accounts are open than that means they're open to the public. It's a public sphere that kind of sucks you in and doesn't let go. It's easy to become subsumed by the sea of information and hashtags, and reporters are no different.

Reporters have their own Twitter accounts and probably follow different people to get leads on stories, while others want the reporters to follow them so they can get their story out to more people. Some stories do get out this way, but many are ignored, or if they do get out it isn't making the difference the Tweeter hopes to make.

But at times Twitter and other social media sites do make a difference. Most of the time we probably don't notice because we don't know what other path we would've taken had we not accessed the information we did to tell the story about whatever major event is being broadcast on Twitter. And each perspective matters.

The events in Ferguson and St. Louis made it clear that what Rebelutionary_Z or Search4Swag saw were definitely not the same thing the mainstream media videocamera operators & editors chose to show us. From one side you could see that tear gas canisters were being used against protesters in residential neighborhoods. Twitter feeds showed us pictures of wounded protesters, and told us of gas being used on babies and grandmas. Smoke was filling up whole blocks where people lived, and later on Search4Swag tweeted out videos of a burning vehicle and building.

On the late night news I watched the two minute clip the station gave space for to show the protest and saw the obvious differences in the portrayal of events. The limited space was used to present the side of the police who had videotaped a protester throwing a brick. The same incident had been tweeted earlier on from the perspective of a protester, but on the mainstream media for some reason it seemed like being hit by a brick was much scarier than being murdered by a cop, for just a moment anyway. But the video also showed the police in a militaristic looking vehicle with a guy in a turret blasting tear gas at protesters. It was a very short clip, but all of a sudden I remembered the picture of the wounded protester and thought, yeah, a tear gas canister would definitely hurt more than a brick, especially if I was wearing riot gear.

The weapon used to fire the tear gas reminded me of the MK19 automatic grenade launcher I shot while serving as a machinegunner in the Marine Corps. It's one hell of a weapon that I certainly wouldn't want to come in the line of site of, even if it was only shooting tear gas.

But that brings me to my point about framing the agenda. Clearly Twitter (and other social media) has worked to frame the agenda in many different instances, but not always in the way people hope or believe it should be framed. The mainstream media just has more reach and they've been in the minds of the masses for much longer, especially the older folks. So how do we use Twitter to frame the agenda the way we want it to be framed?

The problem with that question is the we part, because everybody is different, but the point here is that Twitter is a public sphere - a global digital commons if you will, so there is a we or an us aspect to it, and that shouldn't be ignored. But the I part is important too. For me, I believe it's important to follow people who will fill my feed with important events occurring all over the world who can tell a story from some type of personal or unique perspective that the mainstream media won't give me. It makes me feel more connected to the people who are out there tweeting and livestreaming. But not everything is all good. Some of the stuff on my feed is horrifying, to say the least, but it needs to be there. It's important we don't ignore all the awful things happening in the world. If we did, imagine how much more people would be able to

I C U Hoodie

Only $31

60/40 cotton/polyester fleece, jersey-lined

get away with. Imagine what other pathway our society would follow. In many ways the mainstream media has picked up on this public sentiment. Just showing the image of the police using militaristic equipment to shoot tear gas at protestors gives the impression that the mainstream media does have an interest in providing broader perspectives to the stories they cover. Although their coverage tends to perpetuate the justification of police violence, there is at least some tiny bit of "the other side" being shown on their programs that we can say the agenda is being framed in a way that is inclusive of opposing sides.

But how much of what we see in the news is actually influenced by Twitter? According to researchers Kim Sung-Tae and Lee Young-Hwan, this is called reversed agenda-setting. Reversed agenda-setting is when the common Tweeter posts something that goes viral, which the mainstream media picks up on, and which then has some type of social effect. According to Maxwell McCombs, the agenda-setting theory tells us that, "Through their day-by-day selection and display of the news, the mass media shape our perspectives of the world and focus our attention, influencing our views about what are the important topics of the day." Reversed agenda-setting tells us that the common citizen can also influence the mass media which then influence the perspectives of the masses, and frame the socio-political agenda of the day. Framing refers to the the way in which the information is presented - what information is left out or the level of importance a news organization gives to the event they are covering.

In a 2013 Master thesis by Stefan Volders titled "Agenda-Setting Theory in Political Discourse on Twitter" the author writes in his conclusion, "The findings show that with regards to more political subjects, the public has little influence on the way the news is brought to the people. The public is limited to commenting on the messages that traditional media bring. In this regard, the agenda-setting theory holds. This study further shows that when a subject is more of a public concern and less political, the citizens have more influence on the way the item is brought to the people and how people talk about the subject. An item like this can become so important online that the traditional media eventually incorporate the item on the media agenda. With these subjects, reversed agenda-setting effects occur."

Perhaps this shows that even in a democratic society where the common citizen can contribute to the information the public consumes, there is still a lack of influence by the people on the political agenda. But I'm a believer in what the individual can do and how that can contribute to the collective pathways of all, and don't believe Volder's findings are all conclusive. I believe that

Twitter users do present information which not only influence what their followers are thinking about, but which also shape the way journalists report their stories, political and non-political. But clearly Twitter users and citizen journalist can do far more. But what, and how? How can Twitter users shape the minds of the masses in ways that help us to unfold the pathways we all want to walk upon? How can we frame the agenda for our own personal lives as well as for the community at large?

Well, first off we need more positive information. Stuff that makes us feel good and that makes us want to do something to change the stuff that is bad, for ourselves and for others. We need positive quotes, advice, solutions, and ideas that help us to go down the paths we want to take. If we can do that, if we can find the right information to help us think about the things we truly want to obtain as a society, than we can frame the political agenda, and we can co-create our socio-political realities. We can help to collectively manifest a new agenda for the masses.

This form of law of attraction can be used to shape the lives of large segments of society. We can all feed ourselves with the most beneficial and useful information we can find in order to reshape our collective futures. Of course we don't all want the same thing, and I don't believe we should, but we have the opportunity as a society to do something amazing if we allow ourselves to. I believe we should start with the self. Follow people who can teach you how to do better in school, better in relationships, or who can teach you how to fix a broken toilet, or to sell an old car - whatever it is you want to be better at. Keep at it and keep digging past the fakers and scammers until you have solid sources who can give you timely information. Constantly look for new sources to give you different types of information to open up new pathways and possibilities. We can literally spend a lifetime sorting through information to create new combinations of information just to make the same history we've always made.

But now is the time to rewrite that history. Now is the time to use the information from the past and present to create a new future for all. At one time, the type of information we now have access to for free was considered sacred or taboo. Few people had access to it, but now it's right in your pocket, on your phone. It truly is the information revolution, so lets get to it and revolutionize the way we think about reality. With a simple tool like Twitter, it's all now 100% possible.

References
Volders, Stefan. "Agenda-Setting Theory in Political Discourse on Twitter," Master thesis. Tilburg University, July 2013. http://arno.uvt.nl/show.cgi?fid=130756.

Moon Blankie available at zazzle.com/
distractedmasses

Flower Face design available at
shop.snaptee.co/products/
distractedmasses

Focus or be forgotten design available
at Snaptee: http://shop.snaptee.co/
products/distractedmasses-tbmu8

Cactus & Snow Puzzle available at
zazzle.com/distractedmasses

Relativism vs. Absolutism: Truth in the Making

"Truth is what your contemporaries let you get away with." - Richard M. Rorty

By Rick Albright

Plato presented the dilemma of the absolutism/relativism dyad in his dialogue Crito, a conversation about justice and injustice between Socrates and the wealthy Crito. Socrates is encouraged to escape his execution but, his belief in upholding the law would not allow him to do so. Socrates holds the absolutist position that he will uphold his principles even if it means he will die. This situation is being played out today in American politics where shutting down the government to make a deeply held political belief has become an acceptable tactic. The dialogue develops many of the arguments between the philosophies of absolutism and relativism. Philosophical absolutism is the view that there is an absolute reality which exists independently of human knowledge. Philosophical relativism, on the other hand, advocates the idea that reality exists only within human knowledge, and that reality is relative to each individual.

Absolutism has historically been the dominant paradigm in most world cultures driving politics and driven by belief. The shamans, touched by the supernatural preceded emperor, pharaoh, and king anointed by their gods to lead with divine guidance. If god says it is so there can be no arguments about what should be done. Unless, of course, you don't believe in that god or any god. Then that decree becomes relative to the beliefs of others. Crito, the relativist, believed the law was too harsh and was willing to help Socrates thwart the decree that he die. Socrates, the absolutist, believed that the laws of Athens must be upheld at any cost.

Throughout time history has admired men and women of principle and told their stories as morality tales. Relativism rejects universal truths where truth is transitory believing that moral values should be viewed in context of the environment of the individual and the cultural norms of their society. Promoting one moral truth as superior to all others causes cultural and individual conflicts leading to the violence of suicide bombers and abortion providers murdered by zealots for their convictions as well as, wars between cultures.

The willingness to die for a just cause has long been viewed a virtuous trait but survivors of wars for a just cause often reassess those beliefs. In an article for the Atlantic Magazine, Allen Guelz viewed the civll war through the lens of absolution/relativism and concluded that the violence of the civil war caused the popularity of religious absolutism in the United States to decline. Post-war a large number of men reflected on their part of a struggle rooted in absolutism and began to understand that giving ideas like abolition and freedom the status of truth destroyed a generation. The same dynamic is at play in the Middle East and other parts of the world where opposing ideologies, Sunni and Shite or Kurd vs Turk, declare the truth for everybody, destroying the lives of millions of people with war and intolerance.

"The truth" is under assault by forces that began centuries ago and by current trends in the research of inner and outer space. Although absolutism has been the glue of many societies, the growth of relativism has been inevitable since scientists such as Galileo and Copernicus ventured beyond "the truth" and began investigating both inner and outer space. Perhaps the Age of Absolutism and the excesses of it's monarchs had the same effect on people of that time as the Civil War did in the United States. The Enlightenment and science driven Age of Reason followed the monarchs absolute rule. Western religion went through a period of crisis but, the protestant revolution loosened the grip of the church on curious minds that questioned the way things were. Relativism seems to thrive on curiosity and change. The technology we use today would have been magic to most of the earth's past inhabitants and a testament to scientific method and reason.

Reality is being redefined by studies that reflect a relativist point of view. This has brought about a deconstruction of universality and a closer focus on the individual's role in creating their own reality. Many neuroscientists agree with Debbie Hampton who points out in her blog that the world is constructed by a person's brain. Reality is nothing more than our individual brains' interpretation of the signals it receives as we interact with our environments. Because a being receives so many signals the brain actually predicts and creates much of what is sensed. Quantum mechanics suggests that we perceive at most a tiny sliver of reality, and

Swiss linguist, Ferdinand Saussure believed that language constitutes our world where meaning is always attributed to the object by the mind and constructed by and expressed through language. These findings seem to refute an absolutist view of the world where absolute reality exists independently of human knowledge..

Robert Wright, in his book The Evolution of God, proposes that history demonstrates that once a culture has been defeated by a rival they begin compromising until their religions merge and they believe in the same God. This indicates that the absolute truth, which brought about war between different viewpoints, is compromised once there is a winner and a loser. This also points out that the dyad is not a polar system but, rather a spectrum upon which individuals and cultures fall in different places. Perhaps we are shifting our culture to a point where relativism plays a more important role in providing a viewpoint that can keep us from killing each other before we find a compromise.

References

1. Barry, Peter. *Beginning theory and introduction to literary and cultural theory.* Manchester University Press, 2009.
2. Belief, Max. *The age of absolutism* 1660-1815. Hutchinson & Company, 1960.
3. Guelzo Allen. "Did religion make the American civil war worse?" *The Atlantic*, Aug. 23 2015, http://www.theatlantic.com/politics/archive/2015/08/did-religion-make-the-american-civil-war-worse/401633/.
4. Halvorson, Hans. "In response to the question, What does quantum mechanics suggest about our perceptions of reality?" 2016, https://www.bigquestionsonline.com/content/what-does-quantum-mechanics-suggest-about-our-perceptions-reality.
5. Hampton, Debbie. *How your brain creates your reality, the best brain possible, information and inspiration for anyone with a brain.* 2016, http://www.thebestbrainpossible.com/how-your-brain-creates-your-reality/.
6. Keelson,Hans. *Absolutism and relativism in philosophy and politics.* Irvington Pub, 1993.
7. Plato. (427?–347 B.C.). The Apology, Phædo and Crito. The Harvard Classics. 1909–14, accessed via http://www.bartleby.com/2/1/.
8. Wright, Robert. *The evolution of god.* Little Brown and Company. ebook edition 2009, print.

Edwin Star asked us all

What is it good for?
As he ruminated
about the war
his answer
Was a cry much
Like the raven's
Nevermore
As he wailed with
His guitar that war
Is good for
Absolutely Nothing.
But now I know
That is not true
For sixty percent
Of a budget
Appropriated to
Military needs and wants
Belies the truth behind
What Edwin said.
For War is what
Makes the world
Go round supplying
Jobs and testosterone
Checks so our nationhood
Can be massaged.
While we beat our chests,
Call The Other names,
Bemoan their lack of humanity,
So we can blow them away.

Timelessness of War

No matter how
righteous the war
-people die-
enemies are generated
-for generations-
enemies who grieve for
their mothers and fathers,
eons and daughters
brothers and sisters.
-all killed for the war-

Enemies seek compensation,
time becomes meaningless
in the shadow of revenge
for whom it doesn't matter
who has slaughtered whom,
Just another day of death
as far as it's concerned
redemption's not a factor
once you have a war.

Morality vs legality

Abortion as a legal
Issue is not abut morality
Really it is reality.
For as long as children
Are conceived
And not received
With unconditional Love
As long as they are
Illegitimate
Their mothers will
Perceive no one
Wants them around
as their sisters
In the past they
Will deceive those
Who condemn them
Then clip the bud.

the danger of isolation

the hardest thing
In this world is
to concur with
diverse beings

evolution makes
us wary of those
different from us
In one way or another

we Isolate our souls
from
the beauty of each other

The above poems are by Rick Albright. To view more of Rick's work visit: yrisarririck.blogspot.com. Readers are encouraged to submit their own poetry to *Distracted Masses*. Send your poems in an email to: distractedmasses1@gmail.com.

Truth, Disinformation, and Co-Creation

In his famous work The Allegory of the Cave, Plato asks, "How could they see anything but the shadows if they were not allowed to move their heads?" Those who are not allowed to move their heads believe the shadows dancing on the walls of the cave they are in to be reality, never knowing that there is an entirely different reality awaiting them outside the cave - a truer version of reality than they are experiencing. But the question arises, what is "true" reality?

Those of us glued to our phones and TVs, staring at the constant flow of information we receive, are like the people trapped in the cave, unable to move our heads. What we observe becomes our reality, no matter how distant that reality is from our actual location. We are connected by light speed, able to instantaneously communicate across borders, bringing new realities into our consciousness through our devices and news feeds. But if we look, we'll see there is a whole other reality going on all around us. There is a boy without a phone who simply wants to talk to a real person. There is a homeless person, freezing his ass off with no food who you were completely unaware of because you were scrolling through Facebook. A kid screaming for her momma is ignored as the text messages keep going back and forth. You may be somewhat aware of this other reality, but staring at that little screen just seems so much more important, simply because it is a reality outside the one you're already in.

Perhaps Plato was wrong in assuming the people in the cave truly want to be saved. Maybe when they see the "true" reality they'll just want to try and escape it. So many of us already do, through drugs, alcohol, solitude, books, meditation, social media - things that allow us to see the world around us from a different perspective, from a different point of view. Simply by changing our perspective, we change our reality. But still, is this a "true" reality? If I stop getting my news from anywhere but Fox News will I in turn be living in a different reality that is just as "true" as the one I was living in before? As one of my friends told me regarding a supposed "fake" soccer tournament, "It's only as real as you make it." And I suppose that to be true for everyone.

Disinformation works because of this, because it creates new realities. Humans are susceptible to suggestion, particularly if it is repeated over and over, which is precisely what disinformation artists do - feed our heads with suggestions and lies over and over until we believe it. And as soon as enough people believe it, it becomes a reality, a shared reality. Of course there is great danger to this as often times the reality the disinformation artists seek to create is divisive, violent, and environmentally disastrous, but nevertheless, they make it work. They create an absolute reality for large masses of people, which serves the interests of the disinfo artists who often seek to create a reality of suffering and war. Bombs and missiles reinforce that reality. Lobbyists and lawyers ensure it becomes law. This is absolutism. This is the reality we live in today.

But things are changing drastically. As the population of humans grows, so do the number of ideas we have about what constitutes a "true" reality. The more ideas there are, the more combinations of possible realities we create. When I ignore the mainstream media and filter out other people's ideas about what my reality should be, I start creating my own reality. Am I trying to escape a reality that is more "true" than the one I choose to create? Well, when you can't even tell what is fact or fiction because of the mass amount of propaganda and disinformation in the media, I suppose the answer to that question is no. No, neither realities are more "true" than the other, although I know there is another type of reality out there. There are millions of people who believe the disinformation is the "true" reality, and that is a reality I also have to accept. Their reality is just as real as mine, no matter how much we try to convince each other otherwise. In fact, trying to convince them otherwise only makes them cling to the reality they already know even more so. It somehow reinforces their false convictions when you show them evidence to prove that things are actually contrary to what they believe them to be. So than, does it even matter that people choose to live in these fictional realities?

Why can't I walk around with Google Glasses on, living in a semi-virtual reality at all times? Who cares if Donald Trump really believes the outrageous lies he says? Why bother if someone only views reality through one specific lens their entire life? Maybe we should encourage even more people to shut off the reality around them and to plug into some type of virtual, pseudo-reality. Perhaps it will save us from a lot of fighting to accept that we don't have to have any type of shared reality. To know that there is no absolute truth. No absolute anything.

But that would just be running away from the fact that we do share many common attributes. We are all human, after all, and we do all live on this planet called Earth, which lies in a solar system shared by other planets, in a large galaxy, residing in a vast universe in which all things exist within. We know these things to be true because of our relationships to each other, because of our relativistic realities. Our combined perceptions create new relativistic truths that all together form an absolute reality, albeit one that is always changing. Together, relativism and absolutism live in harmony, but what then does that mean for those of us who want to create our own realities, or for those who want to "co-create" new shared realities?

What it means is that it is all possible. Science fict-

-ion writers perhaps provide the most evidence of this possibility. The writers lived out fictional realities in their heads, imagining the images and interpreting them through their words. Each page they fill is a creation of it's own, each word a symbol of the realities the writers lived in while creating their work. These words are then passed on to the reader who reinterprets their meaning, storing ideas about the storyteller's future technologies in their head, the way they perceive them to be. Collectively, the readers have created a new fictional reality in their own heads, living out the story the writer produced in their own unique, yet shared way. Over time the ideas from within the science fiction writers' work comes to life. People talk about the future technologies they see in their minds, and combining their resources they learn how to create these new technologies. Eventually hover boards and flying cars are the new reality. Teleportation devices and time machines almost within grasp.

Yes, reality changes very fast, and writers, artists, and other creative types have helped to bring on these changes through their works. In three generations we went from not being able to fly, to going to the moon and beyond. In just one generation we've gone from knowing only of the planets in our own solar system, to discovering over a thousand new planets. Yes, reality, our shared reality, is much different than it used to be. But how long can we sustain this change? How long can we keep on creating new realities and still be able to have a common shared reality among us all? Will there be a time when we create so many fictional realities that the "true" underlying shared reality will become indiscernible from the false realities? And once again, what makes those realities more false than any other reality, and should we really care anyway?

I believe we should. I believe the explosion of information and our interconnectedness through new forms of communication and our ever-expanding population make it almost impossible to not care. Even through all the disinfo and lies, the communication devices we now have still allow us to have a shared a reality. A reality that is true to all. Sure, military personnel and corporate employees may have to leave their phones at home, state-run information control propaganda programs will keep many people in the dark for years, and our self-imposed censorship and filters will prevent many from seeing what else is out there, but still, we can't prevent the all encompassing, constant flow of information, from reaching the minds of the masses. Perhaps the "truth" will radicalize some, and perhaps it will only reinforce false convictions among others, but to the open minded individual this information explosion is precisely what connects us and brings us a shared reality among all humanity. When we begin to see the information other people are exposed to we begin to understand why they think the way they do, and why they take the actions they take. Having a common, shared reality is important because it gives us insight into how we can move forward as a species, and not just as a bunch of divided factions warring over false ideologies and beliefs. It allows us to learn from one another and to understand why our beliefs about the ultimate reality are so different, yet it connects us in a way that makes those different beliefs a part of our shared reality. Watching a bomb explode on a Syrian hospital, and the blood and destruction that follows, gives us a taste of a different reality that may seem so distant that it has nothing to do with us. Until the refugees start pouring in. Until retaliatory attacks occur in one's hometown. Until a son or daughter is lost to the war. Then, all of sudden, the reality of those being bombed becomes part of our reality. When we see this death and suffering on our digital devices we bring that reality into

"There is no truth, only perception." Artwork by Alex Albright

our mind. Those who are suffering on the ground in war zones become a part of our consciousness, and a part of the public discourse. To deny this reality, to ignore it and escape into another reality, is just as bad as ignoring your own reality.

Yes, we should put the phone down and pay attention to that deviceless kid, and yes, we should ask ourselves how important other peoples lives are in relation to our selves, and yes, we should manage our time accordingly when worrying about what's going on on the other side of the globe, but we shouldn't just stick our heads in the dirt and try and pretend this other reality isn't going on. Because it does effect us. It does change our own personal realities, even when we pretend it doesn't.

But being aware of this external, separate reality than our own is just part of the bigger picture. It is only a recognition of the state of the past and/or present of those outside our purview. Awareness does not give us instructions on how to move forward in order to change our shared reality in a way which is beneficial to the most amount of people. No single person can give us those instructions, however there are numerous websites which provide tools for those who wish to co-create their future realities together. On the trans4mind.com website Collen-Joy Page writes in her article "Becoming Conscious Co-Creators of Reality" that, "The power to alter collective and external realities is only acquired from the deepest place of peace, wisdom, and love." On another website, monikamuranyi.com, advice is given for "those who are having difficulty co-creating." The advice refers to familiar concepts such as karma and synchronicity. Five suggestions are given to help the "Akashically dysfunctional," but number four particularly stands out. It says, "Drop into your core and become peaceful with all things around you . . ." This point is emphasized throughout the various websites and books one will find on co-creation.

There is something about tuning into oneself and seeking out the love within that brings out higher vibrations of attraction. When one can be at peace with their self and their thoughts, then it becomes much easier to create the reality one seeks. Finding this place of peace and love is the end result for many, as there is no greater goal than feeling content, happy, and peaceful. All other things seem to fall into place once a person has mastered the ability to bring inner peace unto themselves at anytime. Once there is inner peace it becomes much easier to vibrate that peace outward, to attract others who seek similar goals, and who desire to share your reality with you.

This is how co-creation begins. Without the inner peace and the vibrations of love, co-creation becomes impossible. When we try to create realities together without love and compassion people become manipulated, lies are told to serve personal agendas, and false realities are created which lead toward more divisiveness, war, and suffering. People who create their reality out of spite for others, hate for life, or fear of those that are different from them will attract similar vibrations. Their spite will be returned reciprocally, their hate intensified, and their worst fears will seem to come true. This is how our politicians "co-create" our reality for us. This is what the mandate of heaven and manifest destiny provide for us - a false reality in which we allow others to control us through fear, spite, and hate. This is the reality we as humans have been creating on this Earth for many centuries now. We've let the "appointed" leaders, banksters, and religious zealots pave our future pathways for us. They've led us through wars, financial collapse, and immense suffering of all kinds for hundreds of years. The serfs, the proles, the common citizen - they are the ones who bear the brunt of this suffering. They are the ones who've struggled so hard over the years to alter the reality those in power create for them,

and now, finally, the common person is beginning to wake up. They are learning that as individuals they have the power to break the cycle of suffering, and they are learning that together this power is so immense that even the most potent of leaders cannot prevent them from co-creating their future reality in a parallel existence, a more "true" existence than those in power pulling the puppet strings want us to live in.

In chapter one of his book *The Post Reality Society: Truth in the Age of Disinformation* author Ian Mitroff explains how even scientists, who consciously attempt to learn about an objective, all encompassing reality, have core individual beliefs which shape and alter the way they view reality. Mitroff explains that these core beliefs are so important, particularly to the non-scientist, that individuals will defend them to the death no matter how inconsistent their beliefs are with the larger reality around them. Mitroff explains that this external reality only strengthens one's core beliefs, no matter how many times those beliefs have been proved wrong. The more you prove them wrong, the more they think their false convictions are true. Mitroff provides examples of how liberals and conservatives both fall into this trap, with conservatives defending their need to pollute, despite all the evidence which proves they are exacerbating global warming, and how liberal Hollywood screen writers and video game makers will claim their violent works of "art" don't contribute to aggressive behavior, despite the fact that trained social scientists have ample evidence which show correlations between violent media and aggressive behavior. More recently, we've seen this played out in regard to police violence in the U.S. It seems, from my perspective of reality, that when the police are presented with evidence which shows they are acting more violently than necessary, they tend to defend their actions even more so. And when they are not held accountable for their violent actions they point to the people who brought them the evidence, and say, "See, you were wrong. Our reality is right." But to the victim of police violence (I've been one - tased in the head by a plainclothes cop for no reason) the reality is much different. The violence is in plain sight, the injustice very clear, and the coverups and corruption so blatant and obvious it becomes shocking to think no one else sees it. The victim's reality is the more "true" reality, but to the rest of the world, to the people who don't have their eyes open and who believe the disinformation they are fed, to them the police's reality is more "true," and unfortunately that becomes the shared collective reality.

So how do we get around this trap? If the evidence contradicting one's reality isn't presented than they'll never know about it, but presenting the information only makes them cling to their beliefs more. It seems like a lose-lose situation for those who don't have the money or influence to co-create the type of reality that government officials and media moguls can, but there is a way around this.

Step number one is to turn off the TV. The television may be entertaining, but it's not there to serve your interests. It's not there to help you create your reality. It's force-fed information coming from people who want you to help build their version of reality. You probably don't have an erectile dysfunction or restless leg syndrome, but the TV sure thinks you do. And it'll tell you over and over that you do until you believe it. Until you let them manifest that reality in your head. Then, all of sudden, you're buying Viagra and all sorts of other unnecessary items to help complete the reality the corporate vultures & disinfo artists seek to manifest.

The internet is no better in terms of the type of information that is there, but the bonus is you can seek out the specific type of information you want rather than just having to flip the channel until you find something that kind of suits your interests. What the internet does is allows one to find the information they need in order to create the reality they want, and then they can share this information with others who have similar interests in order to help create smaller, shared realities. Of course this only works with others when they also want to have a similar experience as you. If that experience is contrary to their core beliefs they probably won't be interested in the reality you have to share. But instead of trying to prove them wrong, the way to open their eyes to these new realities is to just show them what you already have. Instead of condemning one for their false convictions and trying to convert them, just let them know that there are so many more awesome things out there that they can introduce into their own lives. Show them the infinite amount of possibilities they can also choose from. Show them the alternatives.

When it comes to police violence this is no easy task, but doable. Instead of trying to shame the police for their overly aggressive and violent behavior, they need to be presented the alternatives. They need to be shown that there are other options than just shooting to kill, simply because they feel threatened. One of the problems with this is getting information about those alternative options to the right people. If they are being told over and over that shooting center mass with a deadly weapon is the best way for a police officer to stay safe, then that's what they'll believe, that's what they'll do, and that will be their reality. But if somehow we can get through the information control mechanisms which blind them to the external reality around them, than perhaps that will change. I'm not sure how to convince the police to turn off the TV, and I don't think Twitter storms, mass emails, or even a preacher telling them "Thou shalt not kill" will work. But I do think persistence, creativity, and innovation will pay off. As much as I hate getting tased, I do think non-lethal weapons are part of the solution. I can already imagine future wars where huge mother drones will be sent to shock or stun enemy combats on the ground using some kind of high powered non-lethal weapon. Baby drones will then be sent

to take their weapons from them while they're incapacitated. These type of alternatives to killing are now a very real possibility, but if people keep clinging to their core beliefs, than the new possibilities will never be tested. New realities will never be created. If we keep clinging to the ideas of Mutually Assured Destruction, eye-for-an eye, and profit before people, things will never change. But if we just open our eyes and look around to all the different possibilities, and to the external realities right next to us, then we can find a more common, shared reality that everyone can accept But core beliefs run deep. They're embedded into our DNA and enshrined in customs and traditions. Our core beliefs are our reality, and only we know how to reshape that reality, so if the majority and/or the powerful influencers in this world hold the core belief that killing other humans is a necessary part of life, than that will be the reality for the majority of humans on this planet, including those who don't want it to be a part of their reality. And to me this is why having a "true" shared reality is important. There may come a day when we find the disinfo artists were wrong, and their version of reality never manifested. We may one day find that global warming is true, that violent video games do make children more aggressive, that nuclear weapons don't bring more security to a country, and that killing suspects, perceived threats, and enemies is not the best way to bring order, public safety, or a common peace.

So we can either do something about it, or just wait and find out what type of future realities others will create for us. The decision is up to each individual. If someone doesn't want to co-create a new version of reality than they don't have to. They can choose to live in whatever reality they want. But if enough people co-create a new version of reality, a parallel reality, than the possibilities will open up to more people who may not have seen they had a choice. Because we do have a choice. No matter how many bombs, bullets, or cell blocks absolutists build, they can never take away that choice. I've experienced this first hand, having my reality dictated by the fear these absolutists have created, but they still cannot completely control the way I choose to perceive reality, and I choose to see a "true" reality, a shared reality, that is perhaps more absolutist than the truth the absolutists and disinfo artists lay claim to. Together, we can make that parallel reality even more concrete, and that truth more real. We can do the same thing the disinfo artists do, but in a more honest way. We can bring to life a new reality just as the science fiction writers do. We can write our own futures. We can bring to life whatever our imagination can dream up. We can live our dreams. The future possibilities are limitless.

D1STRACT3D MA$$ES

Science Fiction: A Preview of the Future

Snippets from the upcoming science fiction novel by Distracted Masses:

In The Board Room

"We predict Black Throne's profits will grow 750% faster than Goldman Morgan, the IMF, and all the Rothschild banks put together over the next five centuries using this algorithm," Tom Forge, one of the six board members controlling a majority share of Black Throne's stocks, told the room of CEOs and other major stockholders.

It was the annual stockholder meeting, Dec. 15, 2075. They were in the executive suite of the ECB tower in Frankfurt. Despite the multiple fires blamed on arsonist anarchists, or paid Rothschild resistance members, the ECB continued to grow more massive over the years. After it's initial opening in 2015 when the resistance first tried to take on the oligarchs head on, ECB engineers designed new entryways and special underground transportation systems for it's employees. At first the bankers were worried the resistance was genuine and thought they had a formidable opponent, but it didn't take long for the Rothschild's to pull out the old coercive mind control techniques they were so well known for to recruit the resistance and turn another crisis into a profit. The rest of the bankers caught on quick and each financier faction began mobilizing their own armies of resistors, so they could also bet on all sides of every political battle anyone could ever conceive of. Black Thrown had an edge though, because they just managed the money. They didn't invest it, so all they really had to do was make sure the money was spread out enough to keep all their clients happy.

"Now we also predict major sabotage attempts from the Council of World Business Owners and some social disruptions closer to home, but these will be more annoying than anything and our profits won't be affected," Tom continued.

"Tom," Lorenzo, another board member, interrupted, "What the hell are we doing at the ECB? This is Rothschild territory. We ought to be doing this on our own turf."

Blackthrone's "home turf" was Hong Kong, amongst the towering skyscrapers and graviton suites they owned. Lorenzo knew something was wrong. There were too many hidden variables. Why were the Rothschild's really up to?

"This is simple business," Tom told Lorenzo. "We don't have anything to worry about."

Egypt

"How dare you enter the sacred spacetime of Ra Anu-ka!" he heard a voice bellow through the night. The voice pounded and echoed inside Jack's head, as though vibrating his entire insides and shaking his molecular structure to it's core.

"S-s-s-sorry," Jack stammered. "I don't know how I got here. I'm just a lost traveller."

"All lost souls must return to their home," the voice echoed again, this time slightly quieter than before. "Where are you from?"

"I'm from Earth. From America I mean. The United States of America."

"Than you are in the wrong era," the voice answered back. "America does not exist yet. Come to me. I will take you home."

But before Jack could take a single step he felt himself being raised into the air, a cool breeze swirling around him. He was on the hand of the giant statue and it was bringing him closer to the pyramid and up to the glow. In an instant Jack was staring into a giant grey and yellow eyeball. The eyeball itself was bigger than Jack, almost engulfing him from how close he was. It blinked, and then somehow seemed to scan Jack with just a flicker to the left and right.

"Jack," the bird creature said, "I am Isis. Over there is Ra," gesturing to another bird-like creature across from Jack. "Next to you is Osiris and on the other side is Horus." These are not our real names, but these are the names you know us by from the myths we created your human history from. We are not mythological Egyptian gods and goddesses. We are from a different part of the universe, a different part of the multiverse. We are your creator Jack. The future timelines you've lived on were all created by us, but as you may know by now, those probability paths are but a small part of the ultimate reality. We have constrained your species to a certain perspective for your own protection. We made you to serve us Jack. To build these pyramids, to make your skyscrapers, and to mine our gold. We are your gods. We are Jesus, Buddha, Mohammed, and Confucius. The reason you are here is because we realized there is a glitch in our code and we need you to fix it. We cannot bother with these small tasks, as there is much more important items for us to attend to, but this glitch concerns your species, your human species on your original timeline. You will have to take the patch with you and upload it back where you left off on your original timeline if you want to fix the glitch Jack."

The Helicopter

He heard a muffling sound from around the house. "Huh! What? Is somebody there?" a voice came from one of the back rooms.

"Yeah. John, it's me. Sean, your neighbor. There's been an accident. Are you all right?"

"An accident?" Sean heard his neighbor say from the back room. "What do you mean?"

Thirty seconds later John appeared across the living room in his robe and slippers. "What happened?" he asked.

"Come look," Sean said. "It looks like some type of helicopter crashed. Didn't you hear it?"

"No, no," I was asleep," John said.

"Asleep? How? It woke me up. First I heard the blades. FWUMP, FWUMP, FWUMP! Flying past our house at 5:30 in the morning! I couldn't believe it. My alarm hadn't even gone off yet. FWUMP, FWUMP, FWUMP! And then CRASH!" Sean threw his arms in the air as he said this. "Just like in my dream. Crazy, John. It's all crazy I tell you."

John crunched the broken glass under his slippers as he stepped through the shattered door. "What is this?" the old man asked. John had retired from the Army twenty years prior, but it was still all he talked about, just like the rest of the war vets. He was hard of hearing and a bit slow, but still agile for his age. He looked at Sean and asked, "Did they survive?"

"I don't think so." Sean hit the stop button on his camera, having recorded everything so far. "They shot him down John." Sean said. "It was an ambush."

"What do you mean?"

"I don't know, but I had a dream about this," Sean half made up. "There's someone under my tree in the backyard. I think he's alive, but not the pilot."

"Damn helicopters." John said. "Shouldn't even be out this time of the morning. I bet this is some kind of military operation. One of those war games gone bad."

"Maybe," Sean said as he turned the camera back on, scanning the entire scene , walking through the grass to look for a body. "Look John. There's body parts everywhere. He's a goner. Let's see who this other guy is before the cops get here."

"You check it out," John said. "I'll deal with the cops. They won't even bother with you. Do what you need to do."

With that, Sean hopped back over the wall and threw the hose onto the concrete before turning it off. "No fires," he said, before putting his camera inside and walking toward the other him laying on the ground.

The Patch

"Now you know you're lying to me Sean. You know how it works. You decide what to observe and what information is going in. That information is constantly being regurgitated - in your thoughts, in your words, in your future observations. Yes, what you don't observe still happens, but it's no longer your reality. And who gives a fuck about their reality? Their reality is a sham anyway. Stop worrying about them and their reality and take care of yourself. Control your destiny Sean, and help me to control mine."

"But I feel like we're just talking in circles. What can I possibly observe to help me escape their reality? What can I do to make the words flow the way I want them to?"

"Simple, Sean. Go to the library and find the book I have chosen for you. You will see it when it's there. Read the book and write while you're reading it. It will help tremendously. You already know about the law of attraction and you know it works, so why deny it? Next time you send me off to some crazy timeline make it utopian. Otherwise I'm gonna quit, and you still need me Sean. Even if you have to force it, force it. It's still going to be more free than what others want to force upon you. Now listen up. You have to help me. I need your computer. Let's patch the vulnerabilities in the system."

"But why Jack? Why do we have to fix it?"

"You know as well as I do that if we don't fix it we'll all be destroyed. Look. You can't even control what you manifest, and you're disciplined and well versed in the process. Imagine if everyone else could do it too? They would bring their worst fears and terrors to reality. I mean they already are and look what it's doing. Humans aren't ready yet. We're not mature enough as a species."

"But somehow I am? I don't like it. I believe in freedom of choice. Free will, independence, and individual autonomy over one's own future. Why should I help to install this patch which will prevent that from happening?"

"I already told you Sean. Too much freedom leads to chaos. Chaos is only stopped by force, and if such force is used there will be no freedom. Only the most ruthless of dictators can stop the chaos, and that's not what the world needs right now. The world needs a balance. Order, Sean, isn't about draconian laws and fascism. Order is about preventing the entropy. When you can control the entropy you can control time. And for you, time needs to be controlled. For the rest, it can just unfold the way it always has and no one will notice the difference. For you, however, the change will be noticed, but if you don't install the patch now you'll notice it much more. You will be subsumed by the nightmares and there will be no escape. If you make the change now, you will still have control. You need to do this Sean. So let's do it."

"Fine. You convinced me. The computer is yours," Sean said, stepping away from Jack to clear a way for him to get to work. "Go ahead and patch it, but give it real balance Sean. Make it equal for everyone."

"Okay Sean. I'll do what I can, but equal is not going to mean the same thing for everyone. I'm warning you, the people who benefit the most right now, the super rich, well, they're not going to like it at all."

"Do you think I care?" Sean asked. "Right now, that's exactly what the world needs."

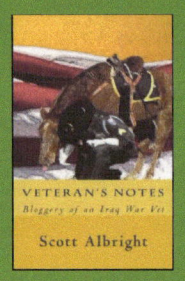

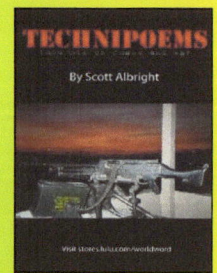

Alien Side Notes

1. **Something or another happened.** Not sure what. Conference, research, proclamation - blinking lights.

   1.1. Streaking lights in the sky. Green. Pleiades Meteor Shower. Saw twice in same area of sky on two different occasions. Very bright, fast moving, long streaks. Large. One seemed to approach airplane and then airplane suddenly not in same location, but still nearby, heading in same direction. Another occasion what appeared to be a star began blinking, moving slowly across night sky. Irregular blink, possibly a satellite.

2. **Many sightings & reportings of lights/aircraft.** (weather balloons/drones)

   1.1. Weather balloons - Spotted and took a picture of a weather balloon to the west/northwest of my house. Was still for a long time, but when daylight came it began moving. I've seen this weather balloon before during the daytime. Also seen clear spherical object in the sky while driving in the Manzano Mountains. Object was clear, but had something dark in the center. Most likely surveillance balloons/UAEs.

   1.2. Drones - Low flying silent aircraft in the mountains and in the city. Extremely low but very quiet. Also, relatives and acquaintances reported seeing drones in the mountains and city.

   1.3. Orbs/Glowing Spheres - Mostly online reports. Unexplained lights appearing & disappearing in the sky. Green lasers/lights coming down from sky at night (beam of light, not natural in origin).

3. **War**

   3.1. Cybersecurity/aerospace/media/police - Russia/U.S./China/India etc . . . (the unknowns).

   3.1.1. Military time travel/teleportation research & experimentation.

4. **Propaganda/Disinfo/Coverups** (most obvious in U.S. police killings of blacks, minorities, poor, etc.)

   4.1. Psychology

   4.1.1. Secret cabals. Corprotocracy, Old Boy Network. Media ownership. Brainwashing (i.e. brand/oligarch loyalty). Statistics, memes, blatant lies/agitators/trolls, repetition of same theme(s).

   4.1.1.1. Xenophobic Nationalist, Nativist, Know-Nothing, Tea Party, Traditionalist, Conservative, Capitalist Corporatists Vs. Multicultural Internationalist, Hybrid, Intellectual, Liberal, Modernist, Democratic Socialist (MNCs vs INGOs).

   4.1.2. Snowden . . . Encrypted alien data. twitter: http://www.theverge.com/2015/9/21/9363863/edward-snowden-alien-encryption

5. **Time travel & teleportation.**

   1.1. National security, privacy, secrecy.

   1.2. Espionage, finance, defense.

6. **Technology**

   1.1. Toroidal engines.

   1.2. Self-organizing, cell-dividing, embryonic, exotic metal shell.

THE HIDDEN DOMAIN BY NORMAN FRIEDMAN

Review By Scott Albright

This book is weird because it makes you feel like you've time travelled back to the 80s. All of a sudden Seth is Max Hedrum and all is a digital manifestation of some other worldly vibration. We are but a consciousness of energy stuck in a bag of skin, on a shell of an earth, spinning off into a holographic spread of two dimensional plasma. Okay, maybe it's not quite like that, but still everything seems quite fantastical, yet somewhat strangely familiar in Friedman's *Hidden Domain*.

This is a book about multidimensionality, quantum mechanics, philosophy, and consciousness. It is old, mostly quasi-scientific hypothesis, and almost too surreal, yet still worth the read.

The *Hidden Domain* isn't some made up fantasy land created by a stoned teenager or lost acid head. No, this book is well thought out, researched, and excellently written, however the ideas are so far from the reality we seem to experience every day that it almost does seem like some type of dream or secondary subconscious thought.

But it's weirder than that. The book itself hid from me for awhile. I accidentally checked it in and then couldn't find it again, only to have it placed on the holds section for me at the library. Having already read most of the book I found it hard to not just skip through different sections, even though that's exactly what I did the first time I read it. Despite that, I always seemed to skip to a section that was pertinent to whatever I was thinking or was going on around me at the time. That type of coincidence becomes fairly normal once you understand the Jungian concept of synchronicity or the law of attraction, but still, this book was weird. It wasn't just normal, ordinary things that would pop up, it was the strange out of this world type of coincidence that is simply unexplainable. For instance, Friedman discusses this hypothesis produced by a strange entity named Seth which says our consciousness, and our thoughts, are energy packets which travel so fast that they go backward in time and then present themselves as the

present which we observe sometime in the future. As I read over this section it became apparent that yes, that's exactly what was happening. My thoughts were moving so fast that they were manifesting themselves in the physical world almost instantaneously. No, not thought out desires or lustful thoughts, although those can come easily too, but the observations of reality itself. Like the thought that I was going to read that section before I skipped to it at random. Or to think someone is going to call and then the phone rings. Were you predicting it was going to happen, or did it ring because you were thinking about the person that called you before it rang? It's hard to tell, but this book made it all the more apparent that these type of coincidences were more than just something metaphysical. Friedman explains something real - abstract - but real. You have to experience it to understand it though.

Friedman does a fine job of explaining all this strangeness, but I don't know if just reading it will bring on the experience. I do know however that the book itself is intriguing. It discusses stuff I really don't know much about but am deeply obsessed with. Time, space, reality, consciousness - these are just some of the ideas Friedman touches on.

If I were a physicist or academic I wouldn't reject the ideas, theories, and findings in this book. There is no doubt Friedman is touching on something quite real, and, as far as I can tell, 100% accurate in all the details and mathematical explanations. I am not a mathematician or physicist however, so I'm not sure how much that means to you, but I will say I'm impressed. Friedman certainly entertained me in a way most authors aren't able to. He really brought the book to life for me, so to speak.

You should read it too, and you can just by going to your local library and finding a copy on the shelves. Or you could visit amazon.com to purchase a copy for yourself and help *Distracted Masses* to earn associate advertising revenue. I hope you choose the latter. It's worth it.

The Dancing Wu Li Masters

By Scott Albright

This book is about relationships - the relationships between time, matter, and consciousness. It is a tale of relationships, and intricate dances, with new and old, east and west, and present and future. Zukav takes readers on a ride through the abyss of the unexplainable world of quantum mechanics, while also exploring the fields of philosophy and cosmology.

He shows how time and space can move forward and backward in logical ways. Using Feynman diagrams, Zukav explains how relationships between the smallest of energy sources can dance around in time as though each moment were but an illusion of our perception, giving the impression that time is but just an illusion as well. This timeless dance of vibrational frequencies permeating throughout the universe is always changing, and yet somehow permanent. As though this dance, this relationship, is the end - the final outcome of our studies of science. There is no reason to dig deeper and analyze the universe piece by piece, as Zukav shows that this will only lead us down a never ending cycle of inconclusive findings, while also blinding us from the bigger picture, which provides a more accurate description of the universe - the description of the relationships themselves, that is.

Analyzing the universe piece by piece is like taking one number out of the entire number system and dividing it in half as many times as possible in order to understand how the entire number system works. In doing this we learn very little about the rest of the numbers and their relationships with each other. We miss the bigger patterns and the ever changing, larger functions of the universe.

But to say that is the end - that it is only the whole, and the relationship between it's parts, that matters - is also a bit of a blinder. This idea that time itself is an illusion may be a false indictment of reality. In studying this relationship between quantum states and macroscopic worlds we come to the conclusion that not only is time a relative illusion, but that it is impermanent - it is not real. The past, present, and future are all bundled into one massive ball of illusory relativity. Time only becomes real to the conscious observer, and then it's only as real as their consciousness will allow it to be - only as real as the observations they make when causing the wave function to collapse.

According to Zukav, "there is speculation, and some evidence, that consciousness, at the most fundamental level is a quantum process. The dark-adapted eye for example can detect a single photon. If this is so then it is conceivable that by expanding our awareness to include functions which normally are beyond its parameters (the way yogis control their body temperature and pulse rate) we can become aware of (experience) these processes themselves. At the quantum level the flow of time has no meaning and if consciousness is fundamentally a similar process, and I/we can become aware of these processes within ourselves, then it also is conceivable that we can experience timelessness."

In section 7, Sutra XVI of the Yoga Sutras of Patanjali it states that "By practicing *samyama* on these three phases, past and future are apprehended as one." The comments below this sutra by Archie J. Bahm state that "Time comes into being in the process of evolution, and the distinction between past and future emerges into experience with the emergence of time. Past and future, thus, are experienced as disturbances in what would otherwise be undisturbed awareness. In order to reachieve such awareness, all awareness of time must be quieted. Then the more ultimate indistinctness between time and the timeless must also be (timelessly) apprehended."

These scientific and philosophical views are in stark contrast to physicist Lee Smolin's idea that time is real - that there is an absolute time, an absolute now, for everyone and everything throughout the entire universe. Smolin doesn't deny the importance of the relationships between the parts of the universe, but his view is much more sobering than that of those who pursue the many-worlds interpretation of quantum mechanics. In Smolin's universe change and cosmological evolution play very important roles in the creation of our own laws of physics, and our understanding of the universe itself. Over time the universe evolves, and as it does our scientific laws must also change. Because of this they cannot be timeless, nor can time itself. To Smolin, Zukav's dance of particles is important, but perhaps not as important as the results the dances produce. That result is that time is real, and perhaps even the most real thing in the entire universe, something Zukav, despite the title of his book, dos not really get into philosophically or scientifically. Zukav does point out the importance of results created by various relationships, but to him they are just part of the timeless illusion we call reality, a reality we might want to reconsider as being not only real, but ephemeral as well.

PAY ATTENTION! Tricks to Stay Focused

1. Physical Exercise

    1.1.   **Yoga -** Join a meet up group. Check out http://yoga.meetup.com/ to find one in your area.

    1.2.   **Bicycling -** Freedom on the road is one thing, but freedom on a bike is something else entirely . . .

2. Mental Exercise

    2.1. Question Your Thoughts - Just because you think it, it doesn't mean it's true. Evaluate your thoughts and ask if there is an alternative way to thinking about whatever is before you.

    2.2.   **Deep Breathing -** Deep breathing, concentration, relaxation. Breathing helps you get oxygen to your blood and brain which prevents cell decay and improves vitality, awareness, and health. Check out one of the many YouTube videos on deep breathing: https://youtu.be/awc8MLSpjlQ

    2.3.   **Calm the Mind -** Find a quiet place near the ocean, or a YouTube video like this one __, and just listen to the waves roll in. Let the waves clear away all thoughts and distractions. Become subsumed by the sound of the rolling waves and let your mind relax and become more attuned to the rhythm of nature. Listen to the sound of your heart and synchronize it with the waves.

    2.4.   **Change Your Neural Pathways -** Reprogram your brain and build new neural pathways by starting a new, healthier routine in your life. Find a bad habit and override it with something healthier and more enjoyable. Read about political or philosophical views on life that are the opposite or different than your own with an open mind and create new ways to think and process information.

4. Emotive Exercises

    4.1 Compassion - Learn to be compassionate toward everyone and everything around you (i.e. the opposition, the cow that made the burger on your plate, yourself, your family, the forest, your home, etc.).

5. Creative Exercises

    4.1 Manifest Reality - From thoughts arise words, and from words arise action. Take the action necessary to fill your mind with the type of thoughts that create the words which make your desired actions occur.

"If you chase two rabbits, both will escape."
- Anonymous

"Any individual can be, in time, what he earnestly desires to be, if he but set his face steadfastly in the direction of that one thing and bring all his powers to bear upon its attainment."
- J. Herman Randall

Quotes fromt http://www.famous-quotes.com/topic.php?tid=227

UFOs: Generals, Pilots, And Government Officials Go On The Record by Leslie Kean

Review by Scott Albright

Leslie Kean's book *UFOs: Generals, Pilots, And Government Officials Go On The Record* is one of the greatest books I ever read. I'm not just a believer now. I have proof. Well, as good as proof I'm gonna get had I been there myself. Leslie Kean brings together top military officials from around the world who've been involved with or encountered strange unidentified flying aircraft in their lifetimes. These are men, all of them, who've been up front in the information battle for the truth about alien existence. Some of them engaged in warfare against these unknown flying vehicles, and some of them attempted to but failed.

Most accounts of these encounters discuss the intelligence of the machines, perhaps with creatures inside, but there is even more to be said about the disinformation, coverups, and first hand accounts of human military to alien engagement than just the strange phenomenon itself. Kean gives us a look into the psychology behind our encounters with these strange machines and our reluctant and stubborn refusal to accept these encounters as part of our human reality. But it's not possible to shove our observations to the side, dismiss all facts, or just ignore the truth - it's right there for us all to see. Kean throws the shit in your face, and there's not much else to it.

We've got to be living on this planet with some strange visitors, or else our best military men and women are all just crazy in the head. They're having hallucinations and dreaming up crazy delusions to mislead the masses, or what they say they've seen and experienced is real . . .

I believe it's real. But at this point it's not about belief. We need proof. Unfortunately this book isn't quite good enough to give us all the proof we need, but it's as close as we're gonna get for a bunch of text and a few insert photos. It's not enough proof - it's just a bunch of views and perspectives, even if they are from the finest minds on the planet. However, these perspectives should be taken seriously, if not for national security concerns, than for mental and physical health concerns, as well for the safety of marine, land, and air transportation systems.

Brazilian Brigadier General Jose Carlos Pereia (Ret.), argues in the book that UFOs *do* pose a national security threat, but few public officials have taken this well respected official seriously. Why? Perhaps because in secret it *is* a national security concern, but if made public the threat to security could be even more of a concern. Perhaps these aren't machines from outer space, but technologies created right here on Earth. If so, government would do everything they could to keep the encounters secret, and spreading disinformation about the technologies themselves would be the first way to go. They could say it was a weather balloon (not a secret atmospheric nuclear testing device), or it was an unexplainable weather event (not a high energy research facility conducting some experiment), or it was it was simply an unidentified flying vehicle, or UFO (not a drone or experimental military aircraft). And who's to say the the military men in Kean's book aren't speaking publicly about UFOs for some ulterior motive? What if they are spreading disinformation to distract us from finding out about their countries' secret military research and technology development? But Kean makes that argument really hard to believe.

Kean, and the military and former military officials writing of their UFO encounters in Kean's book, make me believe what they witnessed was something non-human. No matter how far advanced our technologies have become in secret, I find it difficult to believe we have anything close to what these officials are describing. These flying craft can blink in and out of places in space so quickly that we would have to describe their movement as some type of teleportation or time travel. And some of these UFOs are huge, filled with smaller orb-like craft which have been viewed scouting the skies and reconning human aircraft. Perhaps these are only illusions or holographic weapons meant to deceive pilots, but still, the evidence seems to lean in favor of something else, something extraterrestrial.

Kean doesn't make any assumptions though, and isn't trying to convince the readers that these UFOs are from some other planet, but she certainly makes a case for it. The purpose of the book, it seems, is more about transparency and disclosure. It's about bringing these encounters into the open and discussing them from a rational, academic, and scientific perspective. Kean tells us that the research in the area of UFOs should be taken seriously, not for national security or public health reasons, but because of the scientific advances we could make if we did - because of the collaboration and cooperation it could bring across all fields of study. And because it could help to eliminate some of the mistrust and uncertainty caused by the disinformation and government denials that feed the conspiracy stories and restrain serious advances in international scientific study of these strange unidentified technological phenomenon

Purchase this book using the following link and help *Distracted Masses* earn revenue through Amazon's affiliate program: http://amzn.to/20f1yV1

AL1 3N FAC3S
SKATE DECK

$63.30

zazzle.com/distractedmasses

TAKE US TO YOUR LEADER!

FUTURE WORLD: CREATIVE COMMONS LICENSING

In the past the way people made money was to create something and sell it. The person who created the product took ownership over it with a copyright, trademark, or patent so as to prevent other people from stealing and making money off their product.

Today the rules have changed. Many artists, musicians, writers, and other creators simply can't sell their product when the market is supersaturated. There simply is no demand when customers have an endless supply of free goods on the internet. Need some music? Just download the song. Picture? Right click and save. Need an article? Highlight, copy, and paste. Why pay? It just doesn't make sense.

If you're already rich than I guess it does make sense to continue using the old system where creators protect their products with copyrights and so forth, as it is a perfectly good mechanism from preventing others from stealing your product when enforceable. But if you're an unknown artist with little money for marketing, advertising, or for enforcing copyright laws it simply doesn't work. If nobody has heard of you they won't be able to find your product, and even if they do, why would they pay for it if they don't have to?

So what's the solution? Creative commons licensing. A creative commons license gives artists and creators of all types an opportunity to share their product to the world without having to pay for advertising. It gives them the chance to let others promote their products without having to worry about legalities. The commercial creative commons license is of particular interest to people who want to make money because it offers mutual benefits to creators that other licenses don't. It allows works to be copied, remade, tweaked, and manipulated by others who can then sell that product to earn money for themselves, so long as they attribute the work to the original artist.

Distracted Masses thinks this is a wonderful idea, which is why this magazine is now using a Creative Commons License for all work produced herein. So please use the articles in this magazine to beef up your website or publication. Copy, tweak, and sell the images you find here, or even resell the entire magazine for profit. Go ahead. We want you to.

And in turn we will try to make money off other people's work as well. In the future, you will find articles and works from other creators also using a Creative Commons Commercial license. We want to share what other people are doing and have them share our work in return. We think it will pay off greatly, as this is a mutually beneficial system that will hopefully beat out the old dog-eat-dog winner takes all mentality that has tainted the media landscape for so long. We are believers of the share economy and so we are going to give it a try. If it doesn't work than we're no worse off than before, so why the heck not? We encourage you to do the same and to share what you've created with us so we can help spread the word. Email distractedmasses1@gmail.com to pass on the creative work you want to share in the commons.

Donate

Donations are now being taken at the *Distracted Masses* website and via PayPal. All donations help to support future production of this magazine and research in the social sciences and creative arts. Your contributions help independent media to thrive, while also giving artists, writers, and reporters a chance to express a unique perspective on the discoveries and creations of our time. Visit www.distractedmasses.weebly.com to learn more.

Distracted Masses is licensed under a Creative Commons Attribution-ShareAlike 4.0 International License.

WANT TO CONTRIBUTE?

Distracted Masses wants to hear your story. Send poems, articles, insight, letters to the editor, videos, photos, and anything else you want to share with the world at http://www.distractedmasses.weebly.com/contact.

DISTRACTED MASSES

Albuquerque, New Mexico

Crawling Ant Productions @ 2016

Contributors

- Alex Albright
- James Houston
- Rick Albright

Publisher

Crawling Ant Productions